KEEPSAKE RECIPES
and
FASCINATING FOOD FACTS

Irene Graybill Buckman

Published by
Hara Publishing
P.O. Box 19732
Seattle, WA 98109
(425) 775-7868

ISBN: 1-883697-11-5
Library of Congress Number: 99-071704

Manufactured in the United States
10 9 8 7 6 5 4 3 2

Editing and Recipe Review: Cheri Tucker
Cover Design and Desktop Publishing: Scott Carnz

Dedication

In loving memory of my husband, Frank Buckman, who, along with my children, Harriet and Bruce, have been my chief "taste testers." They were usually appreciative (well, cooks need to experiment!).

For those near and dear to me who may enjoy the memories and ideas captured on paper, I dedicate these Keepsake Recipes to:

...daughter, Harriet Irene Buckman Stephenson, and my son Bruce Frank Buckman.

...grandchildren and their spouses: Misty and David Rookaird and great granddaughter Irene Marie, Tasha Stephenson and Dan Dodge, Matthew Buckman, Mark and Jeni Buckman, and Natalie Buckman.

...dear students from Mapleton High School in Oregon: Florence Camp Lowery, Edward and Jeannette Johnson Wright, June Hall Humphries, Evelyn Collins Doster, Gail Darling Fowler, Lela Maxwell Albert, Evelyn Doster Smith, and Robert Sullivan.

...friends in Walla Walla, Washington including Larry and Helen Buettner, and Larry and Elfreda Shelton.

...friends in California including Irene Johnson, Dorothy Winchell, Jean Lehn, Elsie Glow, Kathryn Pennington, Alice Rickett, Edna Norton, Selma Todd, and Betty Baker.

...special friends met since I moved to Seattle: Bob and Darlene Robbins Erickson and Teeder Mueller.

...to all who have encouraged me to get these recipes and food facts into print. And for you about to read and experiment — Enjoy!

Foreward

Besides being a fabulous cook, my mother knows more tricks about food preparation than anyone. I didn't realize just how clever her tips were until I began to teach my own daughters how to cook. They'd ask me why I kept an apple in the potato bin, for example. I realized I didn't know why. We'd just always done it that way. I'd call mother. She'd tell me the "why." It was to keep the potatoes from sprouting. For every "why" my daughters would ask, I'd respond, "We'll have to call Grandma for the answer."

I realized that what was common knowledge for my mother and was habit for me would need more scientific explanation for my daughters' generation. I also realized that a lot of this valuable wisdom was in danger of being lost.

So in this book, besides a collection of delicious (and award-winning) recipes, are valuable gems that every cook used to know, set down by my mother in her eighty-ninth year. These hints, born out of wood-stove era and gathered over years of listening, reading, and cooking, still serve the microwave kitchens of today and will help you make delicious, safe, and healthful dishes, from the choosing of the best ingredients to the stirring of the pot.

Harriet Buckman Stephenson
June, 1999

Contents

Eggs

Since eggs vary in size, use Grade AA large eggs in all baking recipes unless otherwise specified or an equivalent amount of smaller eggs. A soufflé, for example, can be ruined by the substitution of Jumbo eggs for the Large variety. The former weighs 30 ounces per dozen and the latter only 24 ounces. The difference in egg white volume after beating would be substantial.

One large fresh egg contains:
about 1 tablespoon plus 1 teaspoon egg yolk
about 2 tablespoons egg white

With large fresh eggs:
6 egg yolks=1/2 cup
5 to 6 egg whites = 3/4 cup

Fraction of an egg:
When you want to decrease a recipe and need a fraction of an egg, slightly beat a large egg with a fork. Measure whole—then pour off half—about 1 1/2 tablespoons, for half an egg; and about 1 tablespoon for a third of an egg.

Separating an Egg

When recipe calls for separating the egg, remember to part the yolk from the whites when eggs are cold—right from the refrigerator. Then get the rest of your ingredients together so that the whites can warm to room temperature before beating. (For optimum texture and volume, egg whites should be at approximately 75 degrees before beating.)

The traditional method of separating an egg is to break the shell in half and catch its yolk in the half shell, letting the white fall into the bowl. Transfer the yolk to the other half of the shell, letting the white drain. Repeat until separated. (Note: When separating, if a speck of egg yolk falls into white, lift out speck with an empty eggshell half. If a small amount of yolk gets into white, pour egg into covered container and refrigerate for another use. The addition of even a small

amount of yolk to egg white about to be beaten decreases the volume of the whipped white.)

You can also use your hand as a "strainer" to separate egg yolks from the whites without waste. Crack egg over bowl and catch whole egg in clean hand. Separate fingers slightly to let the white slip into the bowl until only the yolk is left in your palm. It is messy, but you won't break the yolk.

Or a great way to separate an egg easily is to hold a small funnel over a bowl and crack the egg into the funnel; the yolk stays unbroken in the funnel while the white runs into the bowl below.

The stringy white pieces in egg white, called chalazae (kaLAY-Zee), are not imperfections nor beginning embryos, but a natural, edible part of the egg. They serve as an anchor to keep the yolk centered in the thick white.

How to Beat Egg Whites

To beat the maximum amount of air into egg whites, start with whites at room temperature.

A word of warning! Eggs fresher than three days may not beat to highest volume, which is essential in soufflés.

Egg whites should never be beaten until they are ready to be used. If left to stand, the whites will fall apart.

Be sure there is no trace of egg yolk in the whites.

Use any kind of electric mixer, an egg beater, or large wire whisk. The bowl and beaters must be clean and free of grease.

It is always puzzling to know when egg whites have been beaten stiffly enough because most instructions simply say to beat the egg whites until stiff but not dry. An easy way to tell when egg whites are beaten just right is to tip the bowl. When they reach the point where they won't slide in the bowl, they are ready. Also, when beaters or whisk are lifted, the egg whites stand straight and bend just a little. Avoid losing the glossy smooth appearance.

Many recipes call for adding cream of tartar to egg whites when beating them. The cream of tartar causes a chemical reaction, which makes the foam more stable. It is a good idea to add 1/8 teaspoon of cream of tartar for each egg white in recipes calling for separately beaten egg whites.

Sugar makes whites harder to beat; so add it when whites are close to maximum volume. If your recipe calls for sugar or flour, add it very gradually, so that their weight doesn't deflate the egg whites.

Egg whites for meringues, cakes, and some dessert soufflés are usually beaten to a stiffer texture than hot soufflés, because the sugar and some acids like cream of tartar, vinegar, or lemon juice stabilize their volume and structure.

Egg whites for soufflés, omelets, and similar dishes in which egg whites are beaten without binders may result in problems when beaten too stiffly. The egg whites used in latter cases should be beaten to soft peak stage (when whites curl softly when beaters are lifted) when they are still smooth and glossy for easier blending with the batter. If not, the over–beaten egg whites will separate or clump when folded into the yolk mixture.

Egg Cookery

You'll notice when you fry an egg over a conventional burner, the white becomes firm first. That is because it coagulates at a lower temperature than the yolk. The protein in an egg white (albumen) sets at 149 degrees, and the protein in a yolk sets at 156 degrees. By the time the yolk is done, the white has overcooked and hardened. A solution is to cover the pan with a lid. The steam will rise to the top, cooking the yolk more quickly.

But in the microwave oven, the egg yolk, having a higher fat content than the white, attracts more microwave energy and cooks first. Adding other ingredients to the egg dish (even water for poaching) or scrambling the eggs to mix the yolks makes for more even cooking.

Do not soft-cook or hard-cook eggs in their shells in the microwave oven. They might explode and splatter from the pressure that builds up inside the shell with such rapid cooking.

Favorite Ways of Preparing Eggs

According to a survey made by the California Egg Commission, frying is still the favored way of preparing eggs, soft-cooked eggs were second, hard-cooked third, and then scrambled. With present emphasis on nutrition and diet, soft-boiled and hard-cooked eggs are gaining in popularity because they are not cooked in fat.

Fried Eggs

There are a few things to remember in preparing sunny-side up or over-easy fried eggs.

Butter is preferable to bacon grease for frying eggs because the sugar used to cure bacon encourages the eggs to stick to the pan. Use only enough butter to keep eggs from sticking to the pan. A nonstick skillet is really ideal—a skillet just large enough to hold number of eggs to be cooked.

Learning to Like Eggs

When one of my granddaughters was about four years old, she stayed with me while her mother was on a business trip. She simply wouldn't eat an egg. So one morning I tried this method of serving an egg:

To serve soft-cooked egg in egg cup, put egg in cup small end down; slice about 1/2-inch of large end of egg shell so egg can be eaten from remainder of shell with a spoon. To start breakfast off with a smile, draw a face on the shell. Somehow the face always makes the egg taste better, or so it seems.

Coddled Eggs

A coddled egg is an egg cooked soft in the shell; white and yolk the same consistency. It is an egg "betwixt and between"—not as soft as soft-cooked eggs—not as firm as hard-cooked eggs. "Tender eggs"—perfect in texture.

Coddled eggs are cooked by immersing room temperature eggs into briskly boiling water to cover completely and at once removing pan from heat. The pan is covered and allowed to stand 6 to 8 minutes, depending on degree of firmness desired. After allotted time, dip in cold water to stop the cooking. In recipes calling for poached eggs, coddled eggs can be freely substituted.

Distinction Between "Hard–Boiled" and "Hard–Cooked" Eggs

A "hard-boiled" egg is one dropped into boiling water and boiled until coagulated; it is tougher and less flavorful than a "hard-cooked" egg.

A "hard-cooked" egg is one covered with cold water, brought to a boil, covered and pan removed from heat to set about 15 minutes. (And research has demonstrated that "hard-cooked" eggs are preferable to "hard-boiled" ones.)

Perfect Hard–Cooked Eggs

Put eggs in a single layer in a pan and cover them with cold water. Bring water to full boil; immediately cover tightly and remove saucepan from heat. Let eggs stand, covered, 15 minutes. Pour off hot water and run cold water over eggs to stop them from cooking—and also makes peeling easier if eggs are to be used immediately.

These eggs will have no trace of green discoloration between yolk and white (caused by over-cooking).

If there is a possibility of a slight crack, add a few drops of vinegar to the water to prevent the white from leaking out before bringing to boil.

Poached Eggs

The word "poach" comes from the French word pocher which means "to place in a pocket."

Strictly fresh, Grade AA or A eggs should be used. If eggs are not fresh, the whites will flow and spread out in the water when poaching. Before poaching, bring eggs to room temperature either by immersing eggs in very hot water in saucepan for 5 to 10 seconds (lift from pan with slotted spoon and set aside), or put eggs in a bowl and while getting other things together, let hot water trickle on them from the faucet. This brief immersion helps somewhat to set the white, and the egg will poach more neatly. Then proceed with poaching.

Fill wide nonstick utensil so it contains 2 1/2 inches deep of slightly salted water; add 1 tablespoon white vinegar; bring liquid to rolling boil; reduce heat so water barely simmers, then keep at a bare simmer during poaching.

Break egg into teacup; swirl the simmering water in the pan with a wooden spoon and slide egg into center of miniature whirlpool you created. Immediately lift white around yolk with wooden spoon. The whirling water makes the egg round, full, and compact—supposedly no bits of egg white trailing around in the water.

Allow 3 to 5 minutes to poach each egg. With a slotted spoon, gently lift each egg out of the water; place on paper towel to drain. If poached correctly the yolk will be covered completely by the white and the egg will have returned approximately to its original oval shape. If there are any excess pieces of white, trim from the egg to make a nice shape.

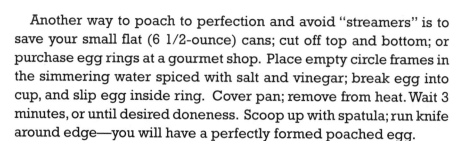

Another way to poach to perfection and avoid "streamers" is to save your small flat (6 1/2-ounce) cans; cut off top and bottom; or purchase egg rings at a gourmet shop. Place empty circle frames in the simmering water spiced with salt and vinegar; break egg into cup, and slip egg inside ring. Cover pan; remove from heat. Wait 3 minutes, or until desired doneness. Scoop up with spatula; run knife around edge—you will have a perfectly formed poached egg.

There is also a helpful gadget on the market for true poaching: a perforated aluminum oval that is immersed in the simmering water; the egg is broken into it and held together in a neat oval shape. There are also nonstick egg poaching pans on the market. The electric automatic egg poacher, by following manufacturer's instructions, is foolproof. The texture of the egg is slightly different—the egg is actually steamed rather than poached—but it is delicious. Or use buttered custard cups for "poaching" eggs. Place egg in each cup and set cup on rack in one inch of simmering water, cover, and steam until desired doneness.

Poached eggs may be done in various other liquids such as milk, consommé, bouillon, soup, tomato juice, mixed vegetable juice, or wine. Just follow the basic procedure for water poaching. The flavor of poached eggs may be enhanced by adding spices or herbs of your own choosing.

Poached Eggs Topped with Creamed Chipped Beef

1/4 cup butter	5-ounce jar dried beef
1/4 cup unsifted all-purpose flour	4 to 6 poached eggs
Dash of pepper	2 to 3 English muffins, split and
2 1/2 cups milk	toasted, or 4 or 6 buttered
Tabasco®	toast slices, crusts removed

In medium saucepan, melt butter. Remove from heat. Add flour and pepper, stirring until smooth. Gradually stir in milk. Bring to boiling over medium heat, stirring. Reduce heat and simmer 1 minute. Add several drops Tabasco® and dried beef. Keep warm while poaching eggs. Lift eggs to toasted muffins. Spoon creamed chipped beef over top. Makes 4 to 6 servings.

Mock Eggs Benedict

4 poached eggs	Cheese Sauce (recipe follows)
2 English muffins	Chopped parsley for garnish
4 slices cooked ham	

Poach eggs or steam (use method desired). Sauté ham slices. Split muffins in half; toast and butter. Top toasted muffins (or toast) with ham slice; top with poached egg and pour heated Cheese Sauce over top. Garnish with chopped parsley. Serves 4.

Cheese Sauce

1 tablespoon butter	1/4 cup shredded Cheddar cheese
1 tablespoon flour	1/4 teaspoon onion powder
1 cup milk	Salt and pepper to taste

Melt butter, stir in flour; blend in seasonings. Gradually stir in milk. Stir in cheese until barely melted.

Omelets

The word omelet, of course, is basic French, while the Italians call their version a frittata.

The French omelet is made with beaten eggs cooked as quickly as possible over high heat. The result is folded quickly and shaped with pointed ends. The center of a perfect omelet is creamy. The French omelet is rarely complicated.

The Italian frittata is generally cooked over low heat in a leisurely manner so it remains flat and round. When ready it is relatively firm but tender to the bite. The frittata may be composed of many things.

An omelet is one of the few meals that requires no advance planning. It largely depends on the moment and the resources of the pantry and refrigerator. It may be a simple affair—a slice of cheese melted into a couple of fresh, creamy eggs—or a complex group of ingredients tucked between the folds of the omelet.

There are really two basic styles of omelets: the classic French, firm on the outside but soft and creamy within, and the puffy variety, which has a soufflé-like texture. The difference is in the method of mixing and cooking. In the classic version, yolks and whites are beaten together and cooked over direct heat; with the puffy omelet, yolks and whites are beaten separately, then folded together and baked. If your omelet always sticks to the pan, try heating skillet over low heat before you add butter and eggs. The results are non-stick every time.

If you use an inside filling, be sure to prepare all the ingredients before starting the omelet. Then when eggs are beginning to set and do not run easily anymore, place filling in line on one side of center and fold other side over carefully so as to form a pouch. To be successful, an omelet must be mellow inside, plump in the middle, and golden all over.

Basic Omelet

2 large eggs	1 tablespoon water or milk
1 teaspoon butter	Filling of choice
Salt and pepper to taste	

Combine eggs, milk or water, salt and pepper; stir together with a fork. Place nonstick omelet pan over medium-high heat until drop of water sprinkled on surface dances around. Add butter to pan and swirl until butter foams but does not brown. Pour in eggs: shake pan gently so eggs slide back and forth over pan bottom. Lift eggs occasionally, using spatula to assist, to allow uncooked egg to flow underneath. Add filling of choice. Tip so omelet rolls over itself and slides onto heated plate.

Plain Cheese Omelet

4 eggs	1/4 cup grated Cheddar cheese
1/4 teaspoon onion powder	Salt and pepper to taste

Sprinkle grated cheese completely over the surface of the half–cooked omelet before folding. Garnish plate with watercress or parsley. (Add flavor by including crumbled bacon pieces with the cheese.) Serves 2.

Chicken Liver Omelet

1/4 pound chicken livers	2 tablespoons sliced mushrooms
2 teaspoons butter	1 teaspoon minced shallots
Salt and pepper to taste	1 teaspoon chopped green pepper

Sauté livers in butter with shallots, mushrooms, and seasonings until delicately browned (just a few minutes—do not overcook). Keep mixture hot.

Make a basic egg omelet. Just before folding cooked omelet, put the liver mixture on one half; fold over; slide omelet onto heated plate. Garnish omelet with watercress and a slice of tomato. Serves 1.

French Toast (For each serving)

1 egg	Pinch of salt
1/3 cup milk	2 slices bread
1/2 teaspoon brown sugar	

Beat egg only sufficiently to combine yolk and white; stir in sugar, salt, and milk. Dip slices of bread in mixture. Fry on medium-hot, buttered griddle or skillet until golden brown on both sides. Serve warm with butter and syrup, powdered sugar, jam or apple sauce.

Oven–Baked French Toast

6 slices bread	1 1/2 cups milk
3 large eggs, beaten	1 1/2 teaspoons vanilla
2 tablespoons brown sugar	Pinch of salt

French bread, sourdough bread, egg bread, raisin bread, or such will work nicely. Butter a 13- by 9- by 2-inch baking dish and arrange bread slices in pan about 1/2 inch apart. Beat remaining ingredients together and pour over bread slices; cover with foil and refrigerate overnight. To bake, place pan on rack in oven; turn oven to 350 degrees; bake 30 to 35 minutes until bread is puffy and lightly browned. Remove from oven and let set a couple minutes before serving. Serve with butter and powdered sugar, syrup, or favorite sauce. (Use 1/2 teaspoon cinnamon in place of vanilla, if desired.) Serves 3.

Biscuits

There are three basic biscuit doughs: milk, buttermilk, and cream. These can be transformed into everything from plain round biscuits to sticky buns, hors d'oeuvres, turnovers, dumplings, etc. Each biscuit has a different characteristic.

It is essential that biscuit dough is not overworked; best results are achieved by minimal kneading. Whether making rolled or drop biscuits, mix dough only until it leaves the side of the bowl; the dough will still be sticky. For rolled biscuits, turn dough out onto a floured surface and knead a few strokes to blend ingredients and make dough easy to handle. Then roll dough to half the thickness you want in the baked biscuits—they will double in size as they bake.

To keep biscuit tops level, press the floured, sharp biscuit cutter straight down without twisting; or cut with firm downward stroke with floured, sharp knife. Use wide spatula or pancake turner to transfer biscuits to baking sheet. To produce soft-sided biscuits, place them close together in shallow baking pan. For biscuits with crusty sides, place them at least one inch apart on baking sheet.

To keep bottoms of biscuits from browning too much, use either a heavy, ungreased baking sheet or two lighter sheets, one on top of other. Do not grease baking sheet, because greasing can also cause overcooked bottoms.

Biscuits Supreme (Exceptionally tender)

1/4 cup Crisco®	1/8 teaspoon salt
1 cup flour	1 teaspoon sugar
2 teaspoons baking powder	1/3 cup milk
1/4 teaspoon cream of tartar	

Cut Crisco® into sifted dry ingredients until mixture resembles coarse meal. Add milk; stir just until dough follows fork around bowl. Pat or roll 1/2-inch thick on lightly floured cloth; cut with biscuit cutter. Bake on ungreased baking sheet in 425-degree oven 10 to 12 minutes. Makes about 8 biscuits.

Fantastic Cream Biscuits

1/4 cup butter	1/4 teaspoon salt
2 cups all-purpose flour	1 cup+1 1/2 teaspoons heavy cream
1 tablespoon baking powder	

Cut butter into sifted dry ingredients. Stir in heavy cream; knead quickly. Do not overwork. Roll 1/2-inch thick; cut into squares. Bake in preheated 400- to 425-degree oven about 18 minutes. Serve immediately. Makes about 12 biscuits.

Sweet Potato Biscuits (Special)

1 extra large egg	1 cup all-purpose flour
1/4 cup brown sugar	2 teaspoons baking powder
2 tablespoons butter	1/8 teaspoon salt
1/2 cup (steamed, peeled, mashed) sweet potatoes	

Beat egg and sugar together until light. In another container, using same beater, beat together butter and mashed sweet potato until smooth. Combine egg mixture and sweet potato mixture; beat until well mixed. Stir in sifted flour and salt; stir only until all flour is blended in. The mixture will be sticky. On lightly floured surface, with floured hands, pat dough into rectangle 1/2-inch thick. Lightly brush top with canned milk or cream. Use very sharp knife; dip in flour and cut rectangle into 12 squares. Place squares on ungreased baking sheet. Bake in upper 1/3 of a preheated 350-degree oven 15 to 20 minutes until light golden brown. (Double recipe, if desired.)

Muffins

Muffin Preparation

Always sift dry ingredients together at least three times. This is necessary because muffins are mixed so briefly. Beat liquid ingredients with rotary beater; but after adding dry ingredients, stir with a kitchen fork—never beat. Mix only until ingredients are just moistened. Batter should be lumpy. Spoon into buttered and lightly floured muffin tins; let stand 5 minutes for liquid to begin reacting with the leavening agents (baking powder or soda). Then bake according to recipe directions.

Apple Muffins

1 large egg	2 cups flour
1 cup milk	4 teaspoons baking powder
2 tablespoons brown sugar	1/8 teaspoon salt
1 cup grated apples	2 tablespoons butter, melted

Beat together egg, milk, and brown sugar. Stir mixture into sifted dry ingredients to moisten. Add apples; spoon batter into well buttered and lightly floured muffin tins, filling each 2/3 full. For a sugar-crust top, sprinkle tops generously with a sugar-cinnamon mixture. Bake in upper 1/3 of a 400-degree oven 20 to 25 minutes until muffins puff high, turn brown, and begin to shrink from sides of pan. Makes 12 medium-sized muffins.

Blueberry Buttermilk Muffins

1/2 cup buttermilk	1 1/4 cups all-purpose flour
1 large egg	1 1/2 teaspoons baking powder
1/2 cup brown sugar	1/2 teaspoon soda
Pinch of salt	3/4 cup fresh blueberries
2 tablespoons butter, melted	

Preheat oven to 400 degrees. Place paper cups in muffin pans. Beat egg, add sugar; beat until light; stir in buttermilk and butter. Stir into sifted dry ingredients just enough to moisten. Gently stir in blueberries. Spoon batter into the muffin cups. Bake on middle shelf in 400-degree oven about 30 minutes until golden brown. Cool a few minutes in muffin pan; then remove muffins to rack. Serve slightly warm. These are also nice the second day, and they freeze nicely. Double recipe, if desired.

Date and Raisin Muffins

1 egg	2 cups flour
2 tablespoons brown sugar	2 teaspoons baking powder
1/4 teaspoon salt	2 tablespoons softened butter
1 cup milk	2 tablespoons chopped raisins
2 tablespoons chopped dates	

Preheat oven to 400 degrees. Sift together flour and baking powder. Beat egg; stir in brown sugar and salt. Add sifted dry ingredients alternately with milk. Add softened butter, raisins, and dates. Beat thoroughly; pour into greased muffin pans. Bake about 25 minutes.

Delightful Multi-grain Muffins

3	tablespoons brown sugar	3/4	cup all-purpose flour
1/4	teaspoon salt	1/2	cup yellow cornmeal
1	cup 1% low-fat milk	1/2	cup quick-cooking Quaker® Oats
1/4	cup butter	3	tablespoons toasted wheat germ
1	egg	1	tablespoon baking powder

Oil and lightly flour 12 muffin-pan cups. Preheat oven to 375 degrees. Measure the flour, cornmeal, Quaker® oats, toasted wheat germ, salt, and baking powder into quart jar; put on jar lid; shake jar up and down and around to thoroughly mix (or blend these ingredients together in a large bowl). Beat together egg, sugar, butter, and milk until well blended. Stir in flour mixture just until flour is moistened. Divide mixture among muffin-pan cups; let set 5 minutes. Bake until golden brown, about 30 minutes.

Buttermilk Oatmeal Muffins

1	cup rolled oats	1	cup all-purpose flour
1	cup buttermilk	1 1/2	teaspoons baking powder
1/4	cup brown sugar	1/2	teaspoon baking soda
1	large egg	6	tablespoons butter, softened
1/4	teaspoon salt	1/2	cup cut-up dates or raisins

Mix buttermilk and oats together; let stand 1/2 hour. Heat egg, brown sugar, and butter together until light; stir into oatmeal mixture; blend well. Stir in sifted dry ingredients just to moisten. Fill twelve buttered, 3-inch muffin cups 3/4 full. Bake in preheated 350-degree oven about 25 minutes.

Refrigerated Bran Muffin Batter (Makes wonderful muffins)

1 cup buttermilk	1/4 cup shortening
1/2 cup boiling water	1 large egg
1 1/4 teaspoons soda	1 1/4 cups flour
1/2 cup raisins	1/8 teaspoon salt
1/4 cup granulated sugar	1/2 cup bran flakes
1/4 cup brown sugar	1 cup Kellogg's All-Bran®

Combine boiling water, soda, and raisins; cool. Cream sugars, salt, shortening, and egg until light. Add sifted flour, buttermilk, and raisin mixture to creamed mixture; add bran flakes and All-Bran®. Pour into quart jar with tight-fitting lid and refrigerate until needed. To prepare, fill greased muffin cups 2/3 full; bake in upper 1/3 of 375-degree oven about 25 minutes until nicely browned. Makes about 16 muffins. (If you want to serve a crowd, make a gallon of batter by increasing recipe by 4 times as much of each ingredient; refrigerate until ready to use.)

Sour Cream Bran Muffins (Very special)

2 tablespoons butter	1 cup dairy sour cream
6 tablespoons Crisco®	1/4 cup brown sugar
1 egg	1 cup all-purpose flour
1/4 cup molasses	1 teaspoon baking soda
1/4 teaspoon salt	1 cup Kellogg's All-Bran®
1 cup raisins	

Cream butter, Crisco®, sugar, and egg until light. Add sour cream and molasses; mix well. Stir in raisins. Sift flour, soda, and salt together; mix in All-Bran®. Stir in creamed mixture, stirring just until moistened. Spoon into buttered muffin pans, filling three-fourths full. Bake at 400 degrees on rack in lower 1/3 of oven 15 to 20 minutes until muffins are done. Makes 16 muffins.

Cornmeal Gems   (Delicious and light)

1 cup milk	1/4 cup all-purpose flour
1 tablespoon butter	2 teaspoons baking powder
1/2 cup cornmeal	1/4 cup brown sugar
1/8 teaspoon salt	2 eggs, beaten

Scald milk; stir in cornmeal, sugar, salt, and butter; let cool. Stir in beaten eggs and sifted dry ingredients. Divide batter among 6 to 8 buttered tuna-can rings on greased baking sheet. Bake in upper one-third of a 400-degree oven about 15 minutes until delicately browned. Delicious hot or when cold. Slice and toast like an English muffin; or slice for sandwiches.

Scrumptious Muffins

1/3	cup sifted flour	1/4	cup corn meal
1/4	cup sugar	1	cup milk
2	teaspoons baking powder	1	slightly beaten egg
1/2	teaspoon salt	3	tablespoon soft butter
3/4	cup whole wheat flour		

Sift together flour, sugar, baking powder, and salt; stir in whole wheat flour and corn meal. Combine milk, egg, and softened butter; add to dry ingredients, stirring just till moistened. Pour into greased muffin pans, filling 2/3 full. Bake in 400-degree preheated oven 20 minutes or till done. Makes 8 muffins.

Popovers and Puffs

Popovers are easy to make, but be sure to serve them piping hot and puffy right from the oven.

They can be baked in the old-fashioned cast-iron pans or individual cast-iron cups, the village baker popover pan, muffin tins, or heat-proof glass custard cups. But remember, if baking in glass, set oven 25 degrees lower than if baking in cast-iron pans.

Excellent Popovers (Use individual cast-iron popover cups)

2	eggs	2/3	cup all-purpose flour
2/3	cup milk	5	teaspoons butter
1/4	teaspoon salt		

Beat together eggs, milk, flour, and salt until smooth; cover and let set at room temperature until baking cups are heated. Place 10 individual (1/3 cup) cast-iron popover cups on baking sheet in 425-

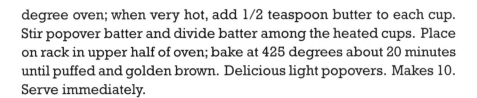

degree oven; when very hot, add 1/2 teaspoon butter to each cup. Stir popover batter and divide batter among the heated cups. Place on rack in upper half of oven; bake at 425 degrees about 20 minutes until puffed and golden brown. Delicious light popovers. Makes 10. Serve immediately.

Cornmeal Puffs (Choice)

1	cup water	3/4	cup all-purpose flour
4	eggs	1/2	cup butter or Crisco®
1/4	teaspoon salt	2	tablespoons yellow cornmeal

Heat water, butter, and salt in medium-size saucepan to boiling. Add the combined flour and cornmeal all at once to butter mixture. Cook, stirring constantly, until mixture leaves side of pan and most of moisture is absorbed. Remove from heat. Add eggs, 1 at a time, beating after each addition until smooth. Drop by 1/4 cupfuls onto ungreased baking sheet. Bake in preheated 400-degree oven about 40 minutes until golden brown and crisp. Make small slit in top of each puff for steam to escape. Delicious served hot with butter. Or cut tops off; reserve; scoop out and discard soft interior; fill with a seafood salad and serve as a main luncheon dish. Makes 10 puffs.

Pancakes

Prepare your favorite pancake batter. Then for perfect pancakes, heat griddle or heavy skillet over medium heat. Test griddle or skillet; it is hot enough for baking when drops of water sprinkled on surface dance in small beads. Grease skillet lightly if not nonstick, then immediately pour sufficient batter from pitcher or large spoon onto greased griddle or skillet to make pancakes the size desired (don't let them get too big or they will be hard to flip). Try to leave some space between pancakes so they won't stick together. Turn the heat down to moderately low and cook pancakes until tops are covered with bubbles and bottoms are brown. Then flip and cook just until undersides are golden brown. Serve piping hot with butter and powdered or brown sugar, syrup, fruit, jam, honey, or other favorite toppings.

For variety, fruits can be added to the basic pancake batter. Apples, for instance, can be coarsely chopped or grated then stirred into the batter. Blueberries can be added whole. Bananas can be mashed and stirred into batter, or a slightly different technique can be used: pour slightly less than usual amount of batter on heated griddle; spread a single layer of banana slices on top of batter and with spoon dribble some batter over each slice; this keeps fruit from sticking to pan when pancake is flipped over.

Apple Pancakes (Delicious)

1 egg	2 tablespoons brown sugar
1 cup milk (minus 2 tablespoons)	2 teaspoons baking powder
1/4 teaspoon salt	3 tablespoons butter, melted
1 cup sifted flour	1 cup grated apple

Beat egg and sugar until light and fluffy. Add butter and milk; mix well. Add sifted dry ingredients; beat until well blended. Stir in apples. Cook on griddle until golden brown on either side. Nice served with butter and powdered sugar, or butter and maple syrup. Serves 3 or 4.

Choice Blueberry or Apple Pancakes

1 1/2 cups buttermilk	3 eggs, separated
1 1/2 cups sifted flour	3 tablespoons melted butter
1 1/2 teaspoons baking powder	2 tablespoons brown sugar
Pinch of salt	1 cup frozen blueberries (or fresh
3/4 teaspoon baking soda	if in season) or grated apple

Beat egg yolks; add sugar and salt; beat well. Add the melted butter (or bacon grease) and beat mixture until light-colored and thick. Add buttermilk and the flour sifted with the baking powder, soda, and salt. Fold in the frozen blueberries (do not thaw). Carefully blend in the stiffly beaten egg whites. Pour less than 1/4 cup of batter on hot griddle for each pancake. When bubbles form, turn and nicely brown on other side. Serve immediately. Perfect with butter and powdered sugar. Generously serves 4.

Buttermilk Banana Pancakes

For quick preparation, mix batter the night before and refrigerate.

1 cup all-purpose flour	2 large egg whites
1 1/4 teaspoons baking powder	1 tablespoon canola oil
1/4 teaspoon soda	1 teaspoon vanilla
Pinch or salt	3 bananas, sliced 1/4-inch thick
1 1/4 cups 1% buttermilk (low-fat)	Powdered sugar for sprinkling
1 tablespoon light brown sugar	over top to serve

Sift together flour, baking powder, soda, and salt; set aside. Beat together buttermilk, brown sugar, egg whites, canola oil, and vanilla; stir in flour mixture until blended. Cover mixture and let set an hour or refrigerate, covered, overnight.

Lightly brush a nonstick griddle or skillet with oil (or coat with nonstick vegetable-oil cooking spray). Preheat skillet over medium high heat. For each pancake, pour 3 tablespoons of batter into skillet. When bubbles first appear on surface, top with some of banana slices. Cook until bubbles cover the surface; flip pancakes and cook about 1 minute. Remove pancakes from pan and keep warm. Repeat with remaining batter. Makes 4 servings (8 pancakes).

Oatmeal Pancakes (An old-time favorite)

2 cups buttermilk	1 1/2 cups uncooked rolled oats
2 teaspoons brown sugar	1/2 cup sifted flour
1/4 teaspoon salt	1 teaspoon soda
2 eggs, beaten	1/2 teaspoon baking powder

Mix together either quick or old-fashioned Quaker® Oats, soda, and buttermilk. Beat eggs until light; stir in oats mixture; stir in sifted dry ingredients. Bake on electric griddle set at 350 degrees. Brown nicely on both sides. Serve with butter and syrup.

Potato Pancakes

4 eggs, separated	4 cups grated raw potatoes
1 teaspoon salt	1/2 cup evaporated milk or cream
1/2 cup flour	1 teaspoon onion powder, optional
Dash of pepper	1 teaspoon baking powder
Pinch of cream of tartar	

Rinse grated potatoes in cold water; then soak in cold water a few minutes; drain and completely dry.

Beat egg whites with cream of tartar until stiff. Using same beater, beat egg yolks and onion powder until light; stir in sifted dry ingredients and evaporated milk or cream; mix thoroughly. Add grated potatoes; mix until just blended. Fold in egg whites.

Drop mixture by spoonfuls onto lightly greased skillet over medium heat. (It using electric skillet, set at 350 degrees.) Cook until a golden brown on either side. Serve with dish of applesauce. Serves 4.

A Version of Jean's Potato Pancakes

6	ounces thinly sliced bacon, diced	2	large eggs, well-beaten
1/3	cup finely chopped onion	1 1/2	tablespoons flour
1/4	cup chopped parsley	1/2	teaspoon baking powder
6	medium-size potatoes, grated	1	teaspoon salt or to taste

Sauté bacon pieces in nonstick skillet until not quite crisp; place pieces on folded paper towels; squeeze out grease. Pour off bacon grease in skillet; then sauté chopped onion until soft but not browned. Cool bacon and onions.

Stir cooled bacon pieces and onions into grated potatoes; add the well-beaten eggs; blend. Stir in sifted dry ingredients and chopped parsley.

Drop batter by spoonfuls onto a very lightly buttered, hot, nonstick griddle or skillet. Brown on both sides. Serve with applesauce. Serves 6.

7-Up® Pancakes

1 egg

1 tablespoon melted butter

5 ounces 7-Up®

1 cup buttermilk pancake mix

Beat egg well; add melted butter; add 3 ounces of 7-Up®; stir in pancake mix; stir in balance of 7-Up®. Makes 8 pancakes.

Zucchini Pancakes

1 egg, lightly beaten	3 cups coarsely grated zucchini
1/2 teaspoon sugar	1/2 cup all-purpose flour
Parmesan cheese	1 teaspoon baking powder
Garnish	Salt and pepper to taste

Combine zucchini and beaten egg; mix well. Stir in sifted dry ingredients; blend thoroughly. Place large skillet over medium-high heat (or heat griddle); oil lightly. Use 1/4 cup batter for each pancake; cook until lightly golden, turning once. Transfer to warmed platter; sprinkle with Parmesan. Serve immediately. These are nice to serve along with bacon and eggs for breakfast. Garnish with tomato slices or parsley. Serves 2 or 3.

Krusteaz® Zucchini Pancakes (Very good)

2 eggs, lightly beaten	2 cups grated, unpeeled zucchini
1/2 cup milk	(the younger the better)
2 teaspoons brown sugar	1 cup buttermilk pancake mix
1/4 teaspoon salt	1/4 teaspoon onion powder

Beat together eggs, milk, sugar, salt, and onion powder; stir into pancake mix; blend. Stir in grated zucchini until blended. Pour about 1/4 cup batter onto hot buttered griddle for each pancake; cook until lightly golden, then turn and brown other side. Serves 2.

Chow Chow Pancakes

1 cup shredded potatoes	2 tablespoons finely chopped onion
1 cup shredded zucchini	2 tablespoons finely chopped
1/2 cup shredded carrots	green pepper
3 tablespoons flour	1/2 teaspoon chicken stock base
3/4 teaspoon salt	Dash of red pepper
1/2 teaspoon sugar	Dash of worcestershire sauce
2 eggs, beaten	

Baking potatoes are best to use because they bind the pancake batter. Prepare all vegetables. Beat eggs; beat in sifted dry ingredients; mix well; pour over blended vegetables; thoroughly blend. Then cook on lightly greased heated griddle as directed in Zucchini Pancakes. These too, are nice served with bacon and eggs. Serves 2 or 3.

Soups

Homemade soup is easy to make and really much better tasting than canned soup. Soup can be made with every category of food: poultry, meat, seafood, vegetables, and even fruit.

Homemade Soup Stock

When you have fowl, such as chicken or turkey, take the skin, bones, and scraps of meat and boil them with a small onion, celery, carrot, some chopped parsley and spices of choice. Add enough water to cover and bring to a boil over high heat. Skim off scum that comes to top, reduce heat to simmer. Cover the pot and let simmer 3 or 4 hours. When goodness is cooked from bones, strain broth into large bowl and let set in refrigerator overnight. Meanwhile pick the morsels of meat off the bones for another use or set aside to go back into the soup. All the fat will come to top as broth cools; when cold and solidified, lift off the fat. (You can reserve and use it as shortening— nice used in making crust for chicken pies; or throw away.) Proceed with type of soup desired; or freeze for future use.

To cook a stock overnight without worrying about it, cover the pot and place in a 225 degree oven until the next morning.

Use the cooking liquid from vegetables or meats as flavorful base for soups or stews.

A good way to thicken a hearty winter soup is to purée a portion of the soup in your food processor or blender. When you stir it back into the pot, you'll have a thicker soup with enhanced flavor and texture.

Main Course Vegetable Soup

Broth from boiled chicken bones, beef broth from roast, beef soup bone, or combination of any

1 1/2	cups uncooked macaroni	1/4	cup snipped parsley
1 1/2	cups sliced carrots	1/3	cup catsup (optional)
1/3	cup sliced onion		Any other vegetable of choice
2/3	cup diagonally sliced celery		Salt and pepper to taste
1	teaspoon chicken flavor base		Diced meat pieces

Cook soup bone or chicken pieces until done. Drain broth and

chill overnight in refrigerator, then remove hardened grease. Cut meat from bones; cut in cubes; refrigerate in airtight container

Bring broth to boil; add macaroni; boil about 10 minutes; then add vegetables of choice and season to taste. Cook until vegetables are just tender. Adjust seasonings. Add a few pieces of the cooked diced meat; bring to boil and serve in heated soup dishes.

Cream Soups
Master Recipe for Cream Soups

3	tablespoons butter	2 cups puréed cooked vegetables
3	tablespoons flour	1 teaspoon onion powder, optional
3	cups milk	1 teaspoon chicken base, optional
	Salt and pepper to taste	1/4 teaspoon sugar, optional

Blend the cooked vegetables in blender to make purée (such as:asparagus, peas, beans, corn, carrots, potatoes, tomatoes) or run vegetables through a sieve. Melt butter; stir in flour and desired seasonings. Remove from heat and slowly add milk, stirring until well blended. Return to low heat; cook until thick and smooth, stirring constantly. Add vegetable puree and reheat just before serving. (Tomato soup is an exception, it should not be reheated.) Adjust seasonings and serve. Broth or consommé may be substituted for the milk.

Seafood Chowders

Seafood chowders are traditionally American, but of all the many types (haddock, shrimp, cod, tuna, clams, scallops, oysters) clam chowder is the most famous. And the chowder war has been going on for as long as there have been a New England and a New York: the New England milk-rich, soft-shelled clam chowder versus the Manhattan with its hallmark of tomatoes and hard-shelled clams.

Both forms of clam chowder are worthy of attention. Clam Chowder is an excellent dish of seductive charm when it is well prepared—either with or without tomatoes that infuriate the Down Easterner and beguile the loyal New Yorker.

Cooks and lovers of clam chowder seem to agree that four ingredients are essential: clams, onions, potatoes, salt pork or bacon.

But whether you use milk or tomato, soft-shelled or hard-shelled, the clam is a born star of stews. You can do almost anything chowder-wise with clams, whether they are butter clams, razor clams, or quahogs (a thick-shelled American clam).

Either canned or fresh clams can be used for a clam chowder. The fresh clams you use will depend on where you live. The large, hard-shell quahogs (called cherrystones when they are small, littlenecks when even smaller) are found from Cape Cod to Texas and from Maine to New Brunswick and often are referred to as chowder clams. Florida has the morton and trading clams; the pacific has Pismo, butter, and razor clams. All are very good cooked in chowder. Northern New Englanders use soft-shell or long-necked clams in chowders, insisting they are the most authentic. Soft-shelled clams are not found south of New Jersey, and the more available hard-shell clams (quahogs, razor, etc.) are perfectly good substitutes.

Today, cooks can choose from evaporated milk, light cream, heavy cream, or milk. Once these are added to a chowder, however, it is important that the dish never be brought to a boil. Today, cream or milk distinguishes a Boston or New England chowder from others; Rhode Island chowders, which may or may not include tomatoes, have a broth base. Manhattan chowder always has tomatoes, never cream or milk.

The Boston Clam Chowder goes better for a main course meal because it goes with wine; Manhattan Clam Chowder is nice as a first course.

Clam Chowder for Two (Delicious)

1 6.5 oz. can minced clams	1/4 teaspoon parsley	
1 cups diced potatoes	1/2 teaspoon Knorr® Aromat Seasoning	
1/2 cup chopped red onion	Juice of half a lemon	
1/3 cup thinly sliced carrots	Salt and Pepper to taste	
1/4 cup diced celery	1/3 cup water	
1/4 cup diced green pepper	1/3 cup evaporated or fresh milk	

Lightly coat nonstick skillet with butter; add diced onions; cover and let sauté a couple minutes—don't brown. Add potatoes, carrots, 1/3 cup water, and drained clam juice. Bring to boil; cover and cook about 15 minutes. Add celery, green pepper, and seasonings. Cook about 5 minutes longer until carrot and potatoes are barely soft. Stir

in drained clams and evaporated milk; heat just to boil; adjust seasonings. Remove from burner; let sit, covered, for a few minutes for flavors to blend.

Oyster Chowder

1 pint oysters	2 cups diced potatoes
3 tablespoons chopped onion	1 teaspoon salt
3 tablespoons butter	1/2 teaspoon pepper
1 cup water	1 quart milk
2/3 cup diced celery	Parsley

Sauté onion in butter until tender; add water, celery, potatoes, salt and pepper. Cover and cook until vegetables are tender. Add milk and let come to boiling point. Simmer oysters in their liquor in a saucepan about 5 minutes or until edges curl. Drain. Add oysters to milk and vegetables. Serve immediately with chopped parsley sprinkled on top. Serves 6.

Seafood

Fin Fish and Shellfish

Of all the foods of this productive world of ours, none has more variety than seafood. Seafood is a delightful change from beef, pork, lamb, or chicken. It is high in vitamins, minerals, and proteins, is packed with great flavor, and has the advantage of fast cooking too. Just about every cuisine in the world has a multitude of ways of preparing fish and shellfish. And there are a multitude of fish and shellfish to prepare. (There are more than 240 species of fish and shellfish on the U. S. market.)

Unlike red meat, fish is not cooked to tenderize it. Fish is tender and free of tough fibers. The result of cooking it is much the same as what happens when you cook an egg: the heat firms the delicate protein. The most frequent error in preparing fish and shellfish is over-cooking. Like an egg, fish becomes tough and dry when over-cooked.

Fish cooked quickly, at a high temperature, will retain its natural flavor and be moist and juicy. Over-cooked fish will lose much of its natural flavor and tenderness. It should be cooked only until its translucent flesh becomes opaque, and the flesh barely "flakes," or separates easily, when tested with a fork. If in doubt of length of cooking time, measure thickness of fish (fillets, steaks, whole fish) at thickest part. Cook fresh fish 10 minutes for each inch of thickness. And serve fish immediately while it is still hot, tender, and juicy. For frozen fish, double the cooking time.

Most cookbooks refer to fish as being "lean" or "fat." Most fish companies classify carp, catfish, codfish, flounder, haddock, perch, pike, red snapper, sole, trout, and whiting as lean fish. Bass, halibut, herring, mackerel, salmon, shad, swordfish, tuna, and whitefish are fat fish.

In general, fish with higher amounts of fat are preferred for baking, broiling, and barbecuing; their natural fat helps keep them moist as they cook.

Steaks, fillets, or small whole fish are easiest to cook when packaged in foil. In each packet add seasonings, a dot of butter or a strip of bacon, a little lemon juice (onion, too, if you like).

Keep in mind one basic rule that pertains to every method, from poaching to broiling to baking to pan frying: Measure the fish at its thickest part (keep a small washable ruler handy), then cook it 10

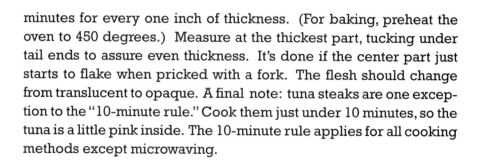

minutes for every one inch of thickness. (For baking, preheat the oven to 450 degrees.) Measure at the thickest part, tucking under tail ends to assure even thickness. It's done if the center part just starts to flake when pricked with a fork. The flesh should change from translucent to opaque. A final note: tuna steaks are one exception to the "10-minute rule." Cook them just under 10 minutes, so the tuna is a little pink inside. The 10-minute rule applies for all cooking methods except microwaving.

Microwaving

Place seafood In a non-metal dish and cover with plastic wrap. Cook approximately three minutes per pound or follow manufacturer's directions.

Pan–Poaching

In poaching, the fish are placed in a single layer in a shallow, wide pan, such as a large fry pan, and barely covered with liquid. The liquid used in poaching may be lightly salted water, water seasoned with herbs and spices, milk, or a mixture of white wine and water, to name just a few. As with other methods of fish cookery, it is important not to overcook the fish. Simmer the fish in the liquid in a covered pan just until the fish flakes easily, usually 5 to 10 minutes. Because the poaching liquid contains flavorful juices, the liquid is often reduced and thickened to make a sauce for the fish.

Compared to classic way of immersing fish in poaching liquid, this technique is a breeze. You cook fresh or frozen fish in a little broth. When it's cooked, remove fish, cover, and keep warm. Boil pan juices down to a succulent sauce; season to taste with salt, pepper, and lemon juice; pour over fish. Serve immediately.

Oven-Broiled Fish

Fat Fish: cut fish steaks or fillets into serving-sized pieces. Clean small, whole fish and remove heads, if you wish. Wipe with damp cloth. Sprinkle both sides of fish lightly with salt and pepper. Arrange fish pieces on a preheated greased broiler pan. Brush with melted butter or equal parts melted butter and lemon juice. Broil 2 to 4 inches from source of heat until pieces are lightly browned and will flake when tested with a fork. Fillets are broiled on just one side; steaks should be turned, basted, then broiled on the other side until browned. Total broiling time is about 8 to 15 minutes, depending on thickness.

Lean Fish: Prepare the fish; sprinkle with salt and pepper and dust lightly on both sides with flour. Place on greased broiler pan; drizzle pieces generously with melted butter; broil until nicely browned on both sides.

Oven-Frying

This method of crisply browning fish in the oven is similar to oven-frying chicken, and offers some of the same advantages. It is quick, requires little attention, and there is no spattering of fat. Serving-sized steaks or fillets of almost any fish or small fish may be cooked this way.

Choose fresh or frozen fish steaks that are 3/4 to 1 inch thick. Dip in melted butter then in seasoned cracker or bread crumbs to coat thickly; place at least 1 inch apart on a foil-lined, shallow, rimmed baking pan. Bake, uncovered, in a 425-degree oven until browned and fish tests done (about 15 to 20 minutes).

Baking

Because fish cooks more slowly in the oven, timing isn't so critical and there is less chance of overcooking. Place the fish (whole or thick steaks or fillets) in buttered pan; add sauce or topping to keep moist; cover and bake at 400 degrees until done. Allow about 15 to 20 minutes for fillets or steaks, 30 to 35 minutes for whole fish (2 to 3 inches thick).

Barbecuing

Fish rich in fat or pronounced in flavor benefit most from barbecuing. Put firm-fleshed fish directly on the greased grill; cubes of these fish hold firmly on skewers for kebabs. To keep tender-fleshed fish from breaking up and falling through the grill, set on greased perforated foil. (If marinating, never marinate fish or seafood longer than 30 minutes before grilling. Oversaturation breaks down the fiber.)

Barbecue when coals are covered with gray ash on grill set 4 to 6 inches above coals. Cover grill with large sheet of foil. Cook, brushing fish often with marinade or lemon butter and turning once with wide spatula, until it tests done. If less than 1-inch thick, allow 6 to 8 minutes total; 1- to 1 1/2 inches thick, allow 10 to 15 minutes.

Sautéing

Heat a small amount of butter or oil with liquid, such as white wine, in frying pan. Add chopped mushrooms, green onions, lemon juice, and seafood to liquid. Sauté over medium high heat until done.

Pan–Frying

One essential is a frying pan that heats evenly. Bread fillets, thin steaks, or pan-dressed fish (thoroughly thawed) by dipping them in a little milk or a mixture of beaten egg and milk then in seasoned flour, cornmeal, bread crumbs, cracker crumbs, or crushed cereal. Let coating dry a few minutes before cooking. Fry fish over medium-high heat in skillet coated with oil (clarified butter is ideal) until golden brown; turn and brown other side, about 5 to 10 minutes depending on thickness. To add variety, embellish it afterwards with a quick sauce.

Deep-Frying

Coat the fish as for pan-frying in your favorite batter mix. Heat peanut oil in deep-fat fryer to 365 to 375 degrees. Lower fish in frying basket into hot oil. When golden brown and barely flakes when tested with tines of fork, remove; drain on paper towels. Fry 1 to 3 minutes depending on thickness of fish. Serve immediately.

Cooking in Foil

Cook the foil-wrapped fish in an oven or a steamer—either way the result is similar to poached fish. Wrap fish in foil, securing it at top to keep in all juices. Place in baking pan (at least slightly larger than package) in a 425-degree oven, or on a rack in a covered steamer over about 1-inch simmering water (185 degrees). Allow 12 to 15 minutes for each 1 inch in thickest part of fish; for unthawed fish, allow 25 to 30 minutes.

Irene Buckman's Salmon Patties

1 1/2 cups small pieces of fresh salmon, skinned and boned

6	tablespoons evaporated milk	Juice of 1 lemon
1	teaspoon Knorr® Aromat Seasoning	Salt and pepper to taste
2	tablespoons fine Ritz® cracker crumbs	Onion powder (optional)
1	tablespoon Miracle Whip®	Extra cracker crumbs
6	slices Oscar Mayer® thin sliced bacon	

Blend ingredients (except bacon) together. Lightly sprinkle 6 circles of cracker crumbs onto waxed paper; then divide salmon mixture evenly on top of circles. Shape into patties; carefully stretch each bacon piece to circle around each patty; fasten each with tooth pick. Sprinkle with very thin coating of crumbs. At this point, patties can be frozen.

Lightly brush both sides with Miracle Whip and bake on steak platter in a 400-degree oven about 20 minutes. If frozen, allow a few minutes longer. (Turn patties about halfway through baking.)

Canned Fish

In using canned fish, the more attractive higher market grades are better for salads or serving plain. For such dishes as casseroles or fish cakes, lower grades will do. They are just as nutritious and flavorful as top quality.

The oil or brine from canned fish adds flavor and food value to seafood dishes. Use the oil, for instance, as fat in the white sauce in making creamed tuna. Brine may be part of the liquid in jellied fish salad.

Store-brands of chunk-light tuna packed in water outsells tuna picked in vegetable oil 4 to 1.

Salmon Substitutions

For recipes using canned fish, try other types of fish. The flavor will vary; you may like the change. If you can get fresh fish, use that, by all means. For substituting canned fish, keep in mind that a 15-ounce can of fish contains 1 1/2 cups coarsely flaked fish plus 1/2 cup liquid. As for the stock, use any flaked, cooked fish or other stock (such as chicken broth).

Baked Seafood Casserole

   4 1/2   ounces large shrimp, deveined
   6 1/2   ounces crab meat
           Seasoned gourmet rice vinegar
           Juice of one lemon
       2   hard-cooked eggs
     1/2   cup chopped red onion or Walla Walla Sweets
     1/3   cup each chopped celery and green pepper
       1   cup milk (1/2 cup evaporated milk and 1/2 cup water)
   2 1/2   tablespoons flour
       1   teaspoon chicken bouillon
     1/4   teaspoon dill weed
     1/4   teaspoon tarragon
           Salt and pepper to taste
     1/2   cup ground Ritz® cracker crumbs
       1   tablespoon grated sharp cheddar
       4   individual au gratin oven-proof servers, shells, or a casserole

If using canned shrimp, drain and carefully run a little cold water through them; then sprinkle on the seasoned vinegar and lemon powder; let marinate while preparing vegetables.

Lightly coat nonstick skillet with butter; add chopped onions; cover and let cook a few minutes—don't brown. Add chopped celery and green pepper; steam a couple of minutes; set aside.

Stir flour in a little milk until smooth, then stir in remaining milk; stir in seasoned base, salt, pepper, dill weed, and tarragon. Cook in microwave, stirring often, until smooth and thickened. Stir the heated sauce into the vegetable mixture and simmer a few minutes. Then drain the shrimp marinade into sauce; simmer. If it seems too thin, stir a teaspoon of cornstarch into a little water and stir into sauce. Adjust seasonings. Stir in crab.

Place drained shrimp in bottom of casserole or divide equally among 4 individual baking dishes or shells. Spoon about half of sauce over top; then top with sliced eggs and remaining sauce.

Combine cracker crumbs and cheese and sprinkle over top. Bake on middle shelf in a 350-degree oven for 30 minutes. Decrease the time to 20 minutes if the individual dishes or shells are used. Serves 4.

To serve: Garnish with a half of stuffed ripe olive in center of individuals, or a sliver of green pepper for color.

Paella

There are hundreds of authentic recipes for the classic Spanish potpourri of meats, seafood, vegetables, and saffron-flavored rice known as "paella." The true Spanish paella was always made with olive oil and saffron (the pollen of the Spanish crocus), which was added to the rice to give it golden color. All ingredients were cooked in a "pallero," the vessel which gives the dish its name, a shallow black iron pan. But lacking a paella pan, the ingredients can be cooked together in a skillet and transferred to a generous lidded casserole with cooking to be done in the oven. The nice part about paella, it can be prepared in advance and reheated to serve.

Rice is the soul of perfect paella. The short-grain rice is used in Spanish paella. Williams-Sonoma and Cost Plus are two sources for Spanish paella rice, generally sold in 2-pound bags. Italian Arborco rice is a good alternative. If economy is a concern, you may choose to substitute long-grain "converted" rice, such as Uncle Ben's® brand. I prefer the converted rice because it holds its shape nicely.

Paella is really a concept more than a set piece. There are so many versions, it is a challenge to work out your own. Do it your way using ingredients that appeal to you. To simplify preparation, have everything well-organized: prepare items in advance—clean seafood, scrub and cut vegetables, and have everything measured, seasonings set out—for efficient work flow. What you feature in a paella is entirely a matter of palate and pocketbook.

Saffron is the world's rarest and most expensive of the spices. The stigmas of the crocus flower are painstakingly plucked by hand; it takes about 75,000 flowers to yield one pound of dried saffron. Fortunately, as little as one filament per portion will give paella its highly distinctive flavor and color. Turmeric can be used if you want to keep the cost down. It doesn't have the same subtle flavor as saffron, but it does give the same bright yellow to many dishes such as paella. You won't need much—only about 1/4 teaspoon ground tumeric for every four servings of rice, added to the cooking water.

Paella   (My version of a company special)

2 1/4 cups rich chicken broth

   I cup Uncle Ben's® converted rice

     Butter

     Salt and seasoned pepper to taste

   1 cup chopped onion

   1 small green pepper, seeded, minced

   1 10-ounce package frozen peas

1/2 cup diced celery

   1 cup thinly sliced carrots, optional

   1 cup 1/2 to 1 inch sliced green beans, optional

   1 5-ounce package Oscar Mayer® Smokies, steamed, cut into 1/2-inch slices

1/6 teaspoon crushed saffron threads, optional

   6 chicken thighs, skinned

   1 chicken breast, skinned, cut into bite-size pieces

1 1/2 ounces can large shrimp, deveined

1/4 cup minced parsley

   2 tomatoes, peeled, sliced into 1/4- to 1/2-inch round slices

     Dill weed

     Seasonings—fresh lemon juice, paprika, salt, and pepper to taste.
     (And excellent for seasoning chicken, Knorr® Swiss seasoning for
     meat; and Knorr® seasoning for fish.)

Heat tablespoon butter in nonstick skillet; add rice and sauté
until rice is golden, stirring occasionally. Add rice to boiling
chicken broth seasoned with tablespoon butter and salt to taste;
bring back to boil; stir; cover and steam over low heat until liquid
absorbed, about 20 minutes.

In same skillet, add about tablespoon butter and the chopped
onions (seasoned with sprinkle of sugar and pinch of chicken bouillon) and sliced carrots. Steam a few minutes; stir and add diced
celery and green pepper; cover; cook a couple minutes. Push
sautéed vegetables to one side in skillet; add a little more butter
and sauté chicken thighs until browned on all sides, season with

Knorr® meat seasoning; steam, covered, on low about 10 minutes. Add the breast pieces, brown: cover chicken with vegetables. Cover and steam about 15 minutes longer.

While mixture is cooking, drain and carefully rinse shrimp in cold water; sprinkle on lemon juice and a little gourmet seasoned rice vinegar; let set. Quick-cook green beans in a little water seasoned with chicken bouillon and teaspoon butter. Quick-cook rinsed peas, seasoned with pinch of sugar and teaspoon of butter. Quickly sauté shrimp in heated teaspoon of butter. Remove chicken thighs from sautéed mixture. Stir in steamed, sliced smokies.

Butter paella pan; spread coating of steamed rice around in pan. Combine shrimp, heated vegetable mixture, parsley, peas, beans, and remaining rice, adjust seasonings. Spread portion of mixture over rice coating in pan; lay on chicken thighs. Top with remaining rice mixture.

Circle top with tomato slices; sprinkle the tomato slices lightly with sugar and dab of dill weed. Set in 350-degree oven until heated through, about 30 minutes. To serve, set in center of table and let guests serve themselves.

Clam Soufflé (An old favorite)

4 tablespoons flour	2 6.5-ounce cans minced clams
4 tablespoons butter	1 teaspoon chicken base
1/4 teaspoon salt	1 teaspoon Worcestershire sauce
1/8 teaspoon pepper	1/4 teaspoon prepared mustard
3 eggs, separated	1/4 teaspoon cream of tartar

Drain liquid from clams; measure 1 cup liquid; save. Melt butter in top of double boiler; stir in flour and seasonings; blend well. Gradually stir in clam liquid. Cook, stirring constantly, until mixture thickens and comes to a boil. Remove from heat. Beat egg yolks until light; stir a little thickened sauce into egg yolks; then blend into sauce, beating until smooth. Add clams. Beat egg whites with cream of tartar until thick, but not dry. Gently fold sauce into egg whites. Turn into 1 1/2-quart ungreased oven-proof casserole. Bake at 325 degrees about 1 hour until puffed and golden. Serve immediately. Serves 4.

Fishing Guide's Recipe for Salmon or Trout

This recipe comes by way of my son, Bruce. He's a trouting guide in the White Mountains of Arizona, renowned for more than 50 trout lakes. When serving trout or salmon for dinner his favorite recipe came from a salmon guide years ago at Campbell River on Vancouver Island:

Take a whole trout or salmon, any size, rinse and pat dry. Cut a piece of heavy duty foil big enough to wrap the fish.

Place fish in middle of foil, underside cavity facing up. Mound up foil to prevent ingredients from spilling out.

Salt and pepper to taste. Fresh garlic to taste. Add pats of butter, margarine, or olive oil (ingredients only in cavity).

Thinly slice a lemon, spread out in cavity. Medium slice a sweet onion (use lots—it goes well on the same fork as the fish).

Pour in either beer (preferred) or white wine, enough to cover up to about 1/3 of the cavity.

Fold foil at ends and top to contain the liquid when cooking. It's okay for steam to escape at top.

Place on medium hot barbecue (preferred) or bake in medium oven. Place on grill with cavity facing up, containing the liquid and cooking thick part most.

Don't overcook! Time depends on fish size. Peek and poke with fork before ready. (1 lb. trout takes about 15 minutes. A medium salmon about a half hour.)

Chicken

When purchasing chicken at the butcher shop, look for a fresh, plump, full-breasted chicken with smooth unblemished skin. The flavor of fresh birds is better than that of frozen birds.

Consider Which Type of Chicken to Buy

A **broiler**, a **fryer**, or what may be referred to as a **broiler-fryer** are one and the same, depending on how your store prefers to label it. It is a meaty, tender, all-purpose chicken that can be cooked in such a variety of delicious ways in less than an hour. It is chicken about 7 to 9 weeks old weighing 2 to 3 1/2 pounds dressed. At the market, boiler-fryers are sold whole, split, quartered, cut-up, and in their particular parts. Broiler-fryers comprise about 90% of all chickens sold.

A **roaster** is a little older and larger than the broiler fryer, about 16 weeks of age and weighing about 4 1/2 to 6 pounds. It is best roasted as its name implies. It has a broad breast and plenty of cavity to fill with a savory stuffing. It is the perfect bird to choose for a festive occasion when the guest list is small.

A **stewing-chicken** is about a 1 1/2-year-old hen, known in the poultry industry as "spent fowl," having reached its peak of egg-laying productivity. It weighs around 4 1/2 to 6 pounds. Because it is older, this chicken is tougher than either the roaster or broiler-fryer, but it still has plenty of flavor prepared by moist-heat cooking methods such as braising and stewing.

A **capon** is a young male chicken that has been desexed. It is fleshy and tender with a high proportion of white meat. A capon can weigh from 6 to 9 pounds. It can be cooked in many ways but is superb roasted.

A **Rock Cornish Game Hen** is a special breed developed by crossing a Cornish game cock with a White Rock hen. It is marketed at 4 to 6 weeks and weighs 1 1/2 pounds or less. It is popular with white-meat lovers.

Pan-Fried Chicken

There are many theories on best way to prepare fried chicken. If you have a favorite method, stick with it. According to tests, whether you moisten or soak the chicken pieces in milk or buttermilk or simply moisten chicken in water before coating with flour seasoned with

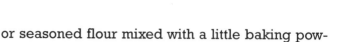

salt and pepper or seasoned flour mixed with a little baking powder, tests prove there is virtually no discernible difference among the various chicken pieces.

Chicken–Fryer and Milk Gravy

1/2 cup evaporated milk	2- to 3-pound chicken fryer
1/2 cup flour	Salt and pepper to taste
1/4 teaspoon paprika	Butter and oil to coat pan

Cut up fryer; place chicken pieces in bowl and pour milk over; turn pieces to completely moisten. Drain over bowl; then shake chicken, two or three pieces at a time, in bag containing the sifted flour and seasonings. If there is time, let dry on waxed paper for half an hour. (Save leftover flour and milk for gravy.) Coat a large heavy skillet (a 12-inch cast-iron skillet is ideal) with thin coating of butter and oil over medium heat. Brown chicken slowly on all sides. Cover skillet tightly; turn heat to low and cook 25 to 30 minutes until chicken is tender and cooked through. Uncover; increase heat; cook about 5 minutes longer to crisp skin. Place chicken pieces on heated platter; keep warm in oven while making gravy.

Milk Gravy

2 tablespoons drippings from fried chicken	1/2 teaspoon chicken bouillon
	2 cups rich milk
2 tablespoons flour	Salt and pepper to taste

Pour off all but 2 tablespoons grease in skillet; stir flour into drippings; let brown nicely before stirring in milk; lower heat; stir in milk. Continue to stir until gravy is creamy, smooth, and thickened. Add seasonings to taste. More milk or less may be used, according to whether thick or thin gravy is desired.

Deep–Frying

The term deep-frying means cooking foods by immersing them in very hot oil. Vegetable oils work best for deep-frying; solid vegetable shortening starts smoking sooner. If oil is hot enough, a crispy shell forms around the food, which prevents it from absorbing oil, seals in natural juices, and produces food that is neither heavy nor greasy. This quick seal can only come about if oil is hot enough. Otherwise the food absorbs the fat, becoming greasy and soggy.

The recommended deep-frying temperature is 375 degrees. In absence of a thermometer, test the temperature of the oil with a 1-inch bread cube; when dropped into hot oil, cube turns a golden brown within 1 minute. If using batter, drop a bit into hot oil; it should sizzle instantly.

Use large tongs or long-handled wire skimmer to add batter or crumb-coated chicken to hot oil, one piece at a time, or lower food basket into hot oil. Avoid overcrowding; all pieces should float freely. Turn as pieces brown. When cooked, remove with skimmer or lift-out basket. Drain food in a single layer on crumpled paper towels, turning once or twice.

Deep-Fried Chicken

3 pound chicken	2 cups self-rising cake flour,
2 cups buttermilk	or all-purpose flour
Salt and pepper to taste	Oil for deep-frying
1/8 teaspoon paprika	

Cut chicken into 8 pieces; rinse pieces and pat dry with paper towels. Place pieces in buttermilk in a large bowl; cover and refrigerate overnight.

In a heavy 5-quart skillet, heat 2 1/2 to 3 inches of oil until very hot (375 degrees).

While oil heats, mix flour, paprika, salt and pepper in plastic bag. Take one piece of chicken at a time, shake off excess buttermilk, put into bag of seasoned flour and shake to coat; lay on waxed paper. Repeat until all pieces are coated.

Fry in two or more batches 5 to 10 minutes (dark meat takes longer), turning chicken as it browns, until golden brown and cooked through. Drain on paper towels. Makes 4 servings.

For deep-frying, remember that hot fat rises several inches when you drop food into it. Choose a pan that is deep enough.

Timetable for Broiler–Fryer and Young Roasting Chicken
Time per pound

Weight in lbs.	Temp.	Time w/o stuffing	Total Time*	Amount of stuffing
1 1/2	400°F.	40 min.	1 hour	3/4 cups
2	400°F.	35 min.	1 hr. 10 min.	1 cups
2 1/2	375°F.	30 min.	1 hr. 15 min.	1 1/4 cups
3	375°F.	30 min.	1 hr. 30 min.	1 1/2 cups
3 1/2	375°F.	30 min.	1 hr. 45 min.	1 3/4 cups
4	375°F.	30 min.	2 hours	2 cups
4 1/2	375°F.	30 min.	2 hr. 15 min.	2 1/4 cups
5	375°F.	30 min.	2 hr. 30 min.	2 1/2 cups

*Increase roasting time by 15 minutes when chicken is stuffed.

Cook chicken to an internal temperature high enough to kill harmful bacteria. Use an instant-read thermometer inserted into the thickest part of the chicken, not touching the bones. Here's what it should register after 15 to 20 seconds:

Whole chicken (insert thermometer in inner thigh area): 180°F.
Bone-in thighs: 180°F.
Bone-in breasts: 170°F.
Ground chicken: 165°F.
Stuffing (cooked in bird): 165°F.
Whole boneless parts: 160°F.

Roasted Chicken

Wash about a 4-pound chicken (fryer preferred) and wipe dry with paper towel—inside and out. Cut out excess fat. Stuff chicken loosely with bread crumb stuffing, raisin corn bread stuffing, rice stuffing, or your favorite stuffing. Pull neck skin to back; fasten with a small skewer. Slip drumsticks under band of skin to secure, or tie the drumsticks securely to tail. Twist wing tips under the back. Place chicken, breast side up, on a rack in a shallow roasting pan; drape with 2 slices of bacon if desired. Roast in 350-degree oven about 1 1/4 to 1 1/2 hours; until tender. Cook giblets separately; chop and use in gravy.

Vegetable Chicken Roasted in a Pot

3 pound broiler-fryer

Salt and pepper to taste

2 teaspoons butter

1/2 teaspoon sugar

1 green pepper, sliced

1 cup thinly sliced onion

3 ribs celery

2 tablespoons chopped parsley

6 carrots, sliced diagonally

Butter a heavy ovenproof 6-quart saucepot or Dutch oven with tight-fitting lid. Layer onion, carrots, celery, green pepper, and chopped fresh parsley in the pot. Sprinkle with a little sugar and salt and pepper to taste.

Wash chicken and remove excess fat; dry with paper towels. Sprinkle inside with salt and pepper; close neck and body cavities with picks or small skewers. Tuck wings under back. Brush with melted butter and sprinkle with salt and pepper; place breast side up on top of vegetables. Cover; bake in 450 degree oven about 1 hour until drumstick moves easily and juices run clear when thigh is pierced. Remove fowl to warm platter to rest a few minutes. Carve; surround with drained vegetables; skim fat from pan juices; spoon juices over chicken. Serves 4 to 6.

Baked Chicken Breasts

6 boneless, skinless chicken
breast halves

1/2 cup grated Parmesan cheese

1/4 cup cracker crumbs

2 tablespoons butter, melted

1 teaspoon dried oregano

1 tablespoons parsley flakes

1/4 teaspoon paprika

1/4 teaspoon salt, black pepper

Mix cheese, crumbs, and seasonings. Dip chicken in butter and coat with cheese mixture. Place in a 15x10x1-inch baking pan sprayed with no-stick cooking spray. Bake in a 400-degree oven for 20 to 25 minutes or until thoroughly cooked. Serves 6.

Turkey

In the early days of this country, Ben Franklin, a great statesman, originally proposed the turkey for the official United States bird. The turkey, however, was not considered by some to be bright or attractive enough for such a distinction. Franklin was really disappointed when the bald eagle was chosen instead. He felt the turkey was a much more respectable bird and a true original native of America.

But Franklin's choice has won its spot. Today the Thanksgiving tables across the country attest to the significant place of the turkey.

Standard Whole Bird

It is always worth looking for a fresh turkey; the flavor is much better than the frozen. But keep in mind, that fresh turkeys, like other fresh meat and poultry, are highly perishable. So for optional safety, buy fresh turkey only if you're shopping within 1 or 2 days of when you plan to serve it. Your market might be able to reserve a fresh turkey for you and hold it for last-minute pickup. Otherwise, you would be smart to purchase a frozen turkey. Remember, when buying a turkey, the bigger the bird, the less the flavor. A 12- to 13-pound turkey, without stuffing, will serve 10 people; with stuffing, 12 people. If you plan to serve more than 12 people, if you want the flavor, buy two small birds rather than one large one.

To figure the size of turkey you will need to purchase, allow 3/4 to 1 pound meat per person for a whole turkey on the bone; with turkey parts on the bone allow 1/2 to 3/4 pound per person; for a boneless roast, allow 6 to 8 ounces per person. And if you want to have some leftovers for other dishes, keep in mind that 1 pound will make about 1 cup of cooked meat.

Prepare stuffing of your choice. Allow about a scant cup of dressing for each pound of prepared fowl. Stuff wishbone cavity of prepared fowl; skewer neck to back. Tuck wing tips behind the shoulder joints. Rub salt in body cavity; lightly fill with stuffing. Use stainless steel skewer nails to close opening or sew up. Push drumsticks under band or skin at tail (or tie to tail).

Brush bird with melted butter, cooking oil, or bacon grease. Place stuffed turkey, breast side up, on rack in shallow roasting pan. Insert meat thermometer in center of inside of thigh muscle, making sure

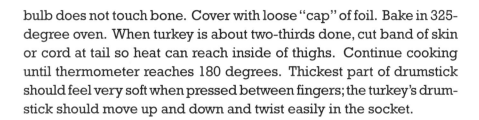

bulb does not touch bone. Cover with loose "cap" of foil. Bake in 325-degree oven. When turkey is about two-thirds done, cut band of skin or cord at tail so heat can reach inside of thighs. Continue cooking until thermometer reaches 180 degrees. Thickest part of drumstick should feel very soft when pressed between fingers; the turkey's drumstick should move up and down and twist easily in the socket.

Turkey Broth

After serving a roasted fowl, such as chicken or turkey, take the skin, bones and scraps of meat and put in a pot; cover with boiling water; season with a small onion, salt and pepper; bring to boil; skim off foam. Then cover and cook until about 1/3 of liquid left. Strain broth into bowl and refrigerate; then skim off fat; freeze broth for future use. This makes a wonderful soup stock and it can also be used as the liquid in your turkey casseroles, adding even more flavor and nutrition. It is a great time and money-saver to have good turkey stock on hand.

Thawing a Frozen, Unstuffed, Raw Turkey

Here are three ways to thaw a frozen, unstuffed, raw turkey. An evenly thawed turkey may be held in the refrigerator for up to 2 days before roasting. Do not refreeze uncooked thawed turkey.

Refrigerator Method: This is the best, although the slowest method of thawing. Place frozen bird on a tray in its original wrapping, refrigerate, and allow to thaw. When partially thawed, remove bag of giblets from cavity and reserve in refrigerator for gravy making or stuffing.

Turkey Weight	Approximate Thawing Time
4 to 12 pounds	1 to 2 days
12 to 20 pounds	2 to 3 days
20 to 24 pounds	3 to 4 days

Quick-Thaw Method: Leave turkey in its original wrap, then place in large kettle and cover with cold water. Change water frequently to speed thawing. Thaw until bird is pliable.

Turkey Weight	Approximate Thawing Time
4 to 12 pounds	4 to 6 hours
12 to 20 pounds	6 to 8 hours
20 to 24 pounds	8 to 12 hours

Microwave Method: If your microwave unit is large enough to accommodate turkey, thaw in glass baking dish, following manufacturer's directions. It may take 1 to 1 1/2 hours to thaw.

After Thawing

Remove wrapping; free legs and tail; remove giblets and neck piece from cavity. Remove any excess fat. Wash turkey inside and out with cold water; pat dry with paper towel. Rub cavities with salt, if desired. Do not stuff bird until just before it is to be cooked.

Testing for Doneness

The most reliable method for detecting when your turkey is thoroughly cooked is using a meat thermometer. The turkey is done when temperature reaches 180 degrees in inner thigh of whole bird in the thickest part of the turkey pieces. Stuffing temperature should reach at least 165 degrees. To check the stuffing, insert thermometer through body cavity into the thickest part of stuffing; leave it for 5 minutes. The stuffing temperature will rise a few degrees after turkey is removed from the oven.

Another method for testing doneness is to press the fleshy part of thigh with protected fingers. If meat feels soft, or if the leg moves up and down easily and hip joint gives readily or breaks, turkey is done.

Doneness can also be detected by inserting a long-tined fork into thickest area of inner thigh. If juices run clear, not pink, the turkey is done.

Roasting Time for Turkey

In order to calculate roasting time, add 30 minutes at end of roasting and before carving to allow juices to settle. Add another 15-minute margin. Since you cannot know the age of the bird and since birds differ in size, shape, and tenderness, use the roasting chart on the next page as merely a general guide.

Type of Turkey	Ready-to-Cook Weight	Oven Temp.	Guide to Roasting Time
Stuffed Whole Turkey	6-8 lb.	325°F	3-3 1/2 hr.
	8-12 lb.	325°F	3 1/2-4 1/2 hr.
	12-16 lb.	325°F	4-5 hr.
	16-20 lb.	325°F	4 1/2-5 1/2 hr.
	20-24 lb.	325°F	5-6 1/2 hr.
Foil-Wrapped Turkey (unstuffed)	8-10 lb.	450°F	1 1/4-1 3/4hr.
	10-12 lb.	450°F	1 3/4-2 1/4 hr.
	12-16 lb.	450°F	2 1/4-3 hr.
	16-20 lb.	450°F	3-3 1/2 hr.
	20-24 lb.	450°F	3 1/2-4 1/2 hr.
Turkey Breast and Portions	2-4 lb.	325°F	1 1/2-2 hr.
	3-5 lb.	325°F	1 1/2-2 1/2 hr.
	5-7 lb.	325°F	2-2 1/2 hr.

Roasting

Place thawed bird, breast up, on rack in a shallow roasting pan. Make sure the rack holds the entire bird above the bottom of pan. Brush bird with cooking oil or melted butter. To use a meat thermometer, insert it in center thigh muscle, making sure bulb does not touch bone. Cover loosely with a foil "cap" that barely touches the bird. Press lightly at ends of drumsticks and neck. Place in 325 degree oven. Baste occasionally with pan drippings, cooking oil, or melted butter.

When bird is two-thirds done, cut band of skin or string between legs so heat can reach inside the thighs. About 45 minutes before turkey is done, remove foil cap to assure even browning. Roast bird until thermometer registers 180 degrees or until the thickest part of drumstick is very soft and whole drumstick moves and twists easily in the socket.

Covered roasting pan directions: Prepare turkey for roasting as directed. Place turkey, breast up, on rack in roasting pan. Brush bird with cooking oil. Insert thermometer. Do not add water. Roast, covered, in 350-degree oven. About last hour of roasting, uncover bird: cut band of skin or string between legs. Baste turkey with pan drippings. Continue roasting, uncovered, until turkey is done. It will not be as golden as when roasted in an uncovered pan.

Foil-wrapped turkey: Wrap turkey, breast up, in greased, wide heavy foil. Place bird in shallow roasting pan without a rack. Place pan in 450-degree oven. Open foil last 20 minutes of roasting to brown bird.

Boned turkey: Remove outer wrapping from turkey. Do not remove inside netting. Place thawed turkey on rack in shallow roasting pan. Insert thermometer. Brush with oil or melted butter. Roast, uncovered, in 350-degree oven. Baste occasionally with oil or butter. Cover bird loosely with foil to prevent overbrowning, if necessary. Roast until internal temperature registers 170 degrees (or follow package directions). To serve the turkey, carefully remove netting and slice.

Turkey halves or quarters: Place turkey, skin up, on rack in shallow roasting pan. Brush with cooking oil. Cap loosely with foil. Insert thermometer in center of inside thigh muscle or thickest part of breast, not touching bone. Roast at 325 degrees until thermometer registers 180 degrees, removing foil last 45 minutes of roasting.

Turkey in the Brown Bag

Prepare fowl as you would for cooking by any other method, salting the cavities, rubbing the exterior of the bird with softened butter. Stuff neck and other cavities with dressing, about 1 cup per pound of dressed turkey. Close by slipping skewers or thin nails through two edges of skin, then lace back and forth with stout string from bottom to top.

Slide turkey into a large, strong, brown paper grocery sack. Twist ends of sack shut and tie securely with string. Place breast side up on rack in broiler pan. Put into 325-degree, preheated oven.

Time carefully. Allow 20 minutes per pound for a fowl over 12 pounds, 25 minutes per pound for a smaller bird. Don't peek! Don't baste. When time is up, lift broiler pan, sacked turkey and all onto top of stove and allow about 15 to 30 minutes for cooling before carving. Some of the juices will have seeped through, but an amazing amount will still be in the sack; so tear it carefully or juices will run all over instead of into pan. Slide turkey onto warm platter.

Oven Cooking Bags

Preparing a turkey in an oven cooking bag is a moist-heat cooking method that produces a moist, tender bird. When using oven cooking bags, preheat oven to 350 degrees. Shake 1 tablespoon flour in bag to prevent bursting. Place celery and onion slice in bottom of bag to help prevent turkey from sticking and to add flavor. Place turkey on top of vegetables; close bag with enclosed tie; make 6 half-inch slits in top to let steam escape. Insert meat thermometer through a slit in bag. When turkey is done, cut or slit top of bag down center. Loosen bag from turkey so there is no sticking; carefully remove turkey to serving platter. (As with traditional oven roasting method, turkey will be done when thermometer reaches 180 degrees.)

Roasting Chart for Fresh or Thawed Turkey Cooked in Oven Bag

Weight (pounds)	Unstuffed (hours)	Stuffed (hours)
8 to 12	1 3/4 to 2 1/4	2 1/4 to 2 3/4
12 to 16	2 1/4 to 2 3/4	2 3/4 to 3 1/4
16 to 20	2 3/4 to 3 1/4	3 1/4 to 3 3/4
20 to 24	3 1/4 to 3 2/4	3 3/4 to 4 1/4

Stuffing for Fowl

Prepare your favorite dressing recipe. For safety sake, never stuff bird the night before or several hours before roasting, as the temperature in cavity remains warm long enough for bacteria that cause food poisoning to multiply. Save time by preparing, measuring, and refrigerating dressing ingredients the night before cooking, but assemble dressing and stuff turkey just before putting in oven. Stuffing should be loosely packed into neck and body cavities. Do not overstuff as stuffing will expand while cooking. Allow 1/2 to 3/4 cup per pound of turkey. After stuffing, tuck drumsticks back into clamp or skin band. Neck skin should be skewered to back and wings twisted akimbo.

To store any leftovers (after bird has been baked and served), remove stuffing from cavity and refrigerate separately.

Bread Crumb Stuffing

1 teaspoon onion powder	2 cups crumbled bread
1/4 to 1/2 teaspoon sage	2 slices crisp bacon, crumbled
Salt and pepper to taste	1 teaspoon chicken bouillon
2/3 cup diced celery	1 1/2 tablespoons melted butter

Combine ingredients. Enough to stuff a 3- or 4-pound chicken.

Potato Stuffing

1 cup bread crumbs	2 cups hot mashed potatoes
1/8 teaspoon pepper	1 teaspoon chicken bouillon
1 teaspoon onion powder	2 tablespoons melted butter
Salt to taste	1/3 cup diced celery, optional

Combine ingredients. Serves 6 to 8.

Sweet Potato Stuffing

1/2 cup butter	4 cups mashed sweet potatoes
2 cups chopped onions	1 tablespoon chopped parsley
2 cups chopped celery	5 tablespoons evaporated milk
1 egg, beaten	Salt and pepper to taste
4 cups cubed bread	

Melt 3 tablespoons butter in skillet; sauté onions and celery until soft. Reserve. Add remaining butter to skillet; brown bread cubes over low heat. Mix together sautéed onions and celery, bread cubes, parsley, salt and pepper. Whip mashed sweet potatoes with egg and milk; stir into seasoned bread cube mixture, mixing thoroughly.

If you have your own favorite mixture for mashed potatoes, potato croquettes, or riced potatoes, you might prefer using that for stuffing. Or, try some flavor additions of your own. Chopped, sautéed mushrooms work well in a savory stuffing. A sweet hint of orange or apple juice, used instead of water or milk as a moistener, is a good flavor complement for turkey or duck.

Cornbread Dressing

1/4 cup butter	1 1/2 cups white bread crumbs
1/4 cup chopped onion	1 1/2 cups cornbread crumbs
1/4 cup chopped celery	1 tablespoon chopped parsley
1/4 teaspoon thyme	1/2 cup rich chicken broth
1/4 teaspoon sage	1 small egg, lightly beaten
Freshly ground pepper	

Toss seasonings with bread crumbs; stir in sautéed onions and celery. Combine remaining ingredients; mix until just blended. Serves 6 to 8.

Raisin Cornbread Stuffing

1/2 cup finely chopped celery	2 cups coarsely crumbled Corn
1/2 cup finely chopped onion	Bread (recipe follows)
1/4 cup chicken broth	I slightly beaten egg white
1/4 cup raisins	Chicken broth
1/4 teaspoon dried dillweed	Fresh herbs, optional
1/4 teaspoon salt	

In small saucepan, simmer celery and onion in the 1/4-cup chicken broth till tender. In a medium mixing bowl combine undrained celery mixture, raisins, dillweed, and salt. Add corn bread and egg white; toss gently to mix. To moisten, add additional broth; toss gently to mix.

Corn Bread

1 tablespoon brown sugar	1 cup yellow cornmeal
1/4 teaspoon salt	1 cup all-purpose flour
1 1/4 cups milk	2 teaspoons baking powder
1/4 cup butter, melted	

Combine cornmeal, flour, sugar, baking powder, and salt; stir to mix well. Add milk and melted butter; stir just until ingredients are moistened. Pour batter into 9-inch square baking pan. Bake in 425-degree oven until center springs back when touched with fingertips, 20 to 25 minutes. Cool in pan on rack.

Oyster Stuffing

1/2 cup chopped celery	6 cups dry bread crumbs
1/2 cup chopped onions	1 tablespoon chopped parsley
1/4 cup butter	3 cups oysters, chopped
2 eggs, beaten	1 teaspoon chicken stock base
1 3/4 cup milk	Salt and pepper to taste

Cook celery and onion in butter until lightly browned. Add crumbs and parsley; mix thoroughly. Add oysters, seasonings, and eggs. Add enough milk or other liquid to moisten.

German Apple Stuffing

1/4 cup butter	1/2 pound white bread cubes
1/4 cup chopped onions	1 1/2 cups chopped apples
1/4 cup chopped celery	1 tablespoon chopped parsley
1 cup milk	Salt and pepper to taste
1 egg, slightly beaten	2 tablespoons raisins

Sauté onions and celery in butter; stir in salt and pepper; pour over bread cubes; add beaten egg and milk; stir to moisten and gently stir in apples and raisins. Spoon mixture loosely into chicken cavity. Serves 6 to 8.

Rice-Vegetable Stuffing

2 small carrots, grated	1 cup long-grain white rice
1/2 cup chopped onions	2 1/4 cups broth (or 2 1/4 cups
1/2 cup diced celery	water and teaspoon chicken
1 4-ounce can mushrooms	bouillon)
2 tablespoons butter	Pinch of sugar, salt, and pepper

Add rice to boiling broth or seasoned water. As soon as boiling, stir; turn burner to low; cover and steam until liquid is absorbed, about 15 minutes. While rice is cooking, sauté onions, carrots, and celery in skillet until barely tender; stir in mushrooms; season with pinch of sugar, salt and pepper to taste. Carefully stir in steamed rice. Adjust seasonings. Spoon mixture loosely into fowl cavity. Serves 6 to 8.

Sauces for Fowl

Cranberry Sauce

Boil 2 cups sugar and 2 cups water 5 minutes. Add 4 cups fresh cranberries and boil without stirring 5 minutes or until all the skins pop open. Remove from heat and let cool in pan. You can also mix this with drained pineapple bits. Makes 1 quart.

Cranberry and Orange Sauce

2 cups raw cranberries (or frozen)

3/4 cup sugar or to taste

1 tablespoon grated fresh orange peel or 1 teaspoon Shilling's® Orange Peel

1/2 cup orange juice

Dissolve sugar in orange juice in casserole dish; add cranberries and orange peel: cover. Microwave on HIGH 8 to 10 minutes, stirring 2 or 3 times. (Berries should pop and mixture boil.) Rest, covered, 10 minutes.

Raisin Sauce

1/2 cup brown sugar	1/4 teaspoon ground lemon peel
2 tablespoons cornstarch	2 tablespoons lemon juice
1 teaspoon prepared mustard	2 tablespoons vinegar
1 1/2 cups water	1/2 cup raisins

Mix brown sugar, cornstarch, and mustard in 1 1/2-quart saucepan. Mix water, lemon peel, lemon juice and vinegar; gradually stir into sugar mixture. Cook over low heat, stirring constantly, until mixture thickens. Stir in raisins. Makes about 2 cups sauce.

Fresh Ground Turkey

Dishes that traditionally use ground beef can be converted to lean ground turkey. Cooking time for ground beef and ground turkey is approximately the same.

Ground turkey is 100-percent turkey (primarily dark meat with some skin) and contains no giblets, preservatives, or other ingredients. It is high in protein, low in cholesterol, with only 8-percent to 15-percent fat.

Ground turkey is much leaner than ground beef and has a mild flavor that does beautifully in a variety of dishes. Ground turkey's delicate flavor readily accepts flavor from seasonings, herbs, and sauces. It can be used for patties, meatballs, meat loaf, burgers, etc. In meat loaf, the cooked turkey holds its shape and is much nicer to slice. And the cost is quite an item: a lean pound of turkey costs less than a pound of cheapest cut of ground beef. You are paying for almost pure protein with no wasted fat content.

It is available fresh or frozen in tray packs or frozen in 1 or 2-pound tubes. If frozen, it should be thawed overnight in the refrigerator, then used within 1 or 2 days, like any ground meat.

Meatball Dumplings

1/4 cup flour	1 pound very lean ground turkey
1/2 teaspoon salt	2 eggs, slightly beaten
1/8 teaspoon pepper	1 teaspoon onion powder
1 teaspoon chopped parsley	

Combine all ingredients lightly but thoroughly with fork. Shape into tiny meatballs (rounded teaspoonful). Drop gently into boiling broth. Set to simmer, covered, and cook about 10 minutes. Serves 4.

Or add to broth when adding vegetables and noodles to make vegetable soup. To use in cream soups, boil dumplings in salted water; remove with slotted spoon to bowl; keep warm. To serve, add 3 or 4 to each bowl and pour heated cream soup over.

Frosted Turkey Loaf

1 1/2 pounds ground turkey	2/3 cup soda cracker crumbs
1 egg, slightly beaten	1/4 cup minced onion
1/2 teaspoon salt	1 tablespoon minced parsley
1/8 teaspoon pepper	1/4 teaspoon ground sage
1/2 cup milk	Frosting (recipe follows)

Combine cracker crumbs, ground turkey, egg, salt, pepper, milk, onion, parsley, and sage. Mix well. Turn into 8x4-inch loaf pan. Spread frosting over turkey loaf. Bake on middle shelf in a 350-degree oven about 1 1/4 hours. Serves 4.

Frosting

3 tablespoons brown sugar	1/4 teaspoon ground nutmeg
1/4 cup catsup	1 teaspoon prepared mustard

Combine brown sugar, nutmeg, catsup and mustard. Mix well.

Pork

The phrase, "Bringing home the bacon," today really implies "Bringing home the pay check." Originally, the phrase meant bringing home the pig, itself. At rural fairs there was the practice of awarding the pig to the winner of the greased pig contest. The person catching the slippery hog was actually bringing home the bacon.

Pork is a nutritious and tasty meat that adds a great variety to meals, but it must be handled properly to make sure it is safe to eat. The food Safety and Inspection Service recommends cooking pork to an internal temperature of 160 degrees.

FSIS officials note that trichinella spiralis, a parasite that may be present in 0.1 percent of the pork supply, is destroyed instantly at 137 degrees.

The National Pork Producers Council recommends the following times for cooking pork: Cutlets and thin (3/8-inch) pork chops should cook to a tender, juicy stage in 10 to 15 minutes. Thicker (1-inch) chops will cook in 15 to 20 minutes. And a pork roast should be taken from the oven or grill when the internal temperature reaches 155 degrees, as it will continue to cook before slicing.

In packing plants operating under federal meat inspection, pork products that may be eaten without further cooking are processed to kill tricilinac—by cooking, special freezing and holding, or curing. All hot dogs and some hams on the market are fully cooked. But before eating any pork product, make certain it is labeled "fully cooked," or otherwise cook it.

Pork comes in many shapes and has a flavor to fit most any occasion and appetite.

Pork Roast

For a perfect pork roast, rub pork with seasoning (salt, pepper, thyme); place roast in shallow open pan; then insert a roast-meat thermometer into center of meat, away from fat and bones. A thermometer is important. It is the only way to tell when a roast is done—and over cooking will dry out the meat. Roasted at a low 325 degrees keeps meat moist and minimizes shrinkage. (A 5-pound roast will produce about 2 1/2 pounds cooked lean meat—enough for 8 to 10 people.)

It isn't necessary to preheat an oven for roasting. Also unnecessary: searing at high temperatures or frequent basting. Do not add water; do not cover. When meat thermometer registers 155, five degrees below the "done" temperature, remove roast from oven as it will continue to cook with its own heat. Let meat rest 10 to 15 minutes before carving. Allowing it to stand sets the juices and makes carving easier.

Baked Breaded Pork Chops

8 lean pork chops	Fine Ritz® cracker crumbs
Evaporated milk	1 (10 3/4-oz.) can cream of
Onion powder	mushroom soup
Butter	Salt, pepper, and sugar to taste

Dip pork chops in milk, then in cracker crumbs; sauté in butter. Place in buttered baking pan; top with cream of mushroom soup; season with salt, pepper, sugar, and onion powder. Cover and bake at 325 degrees 1 hour. Uncover; turn chops; bake until tender. Serves 8.

Pocketbook Pork Chops

1 4-ounce can mushrooms	6 loin pork chops, cut 1-inch thick
2 tablespoons butter	1/2 cup thinly sliced celery
1/4 teaspoon sugar	1/4 teaspoon mixed salad herbs
1 egg, beaten	1 tablespoon chopped parsley
1 cup cooked rice	1/2 teaspoon chicken bouillon
Evaporated milk	Cracker crumbs

Trim off excess fat from chops and make a slit in each to form a pocket. Sauté the chopped mushrooms and celery in butter; stir in beaten egg and cooked rice. Spoon about 1/3 cup or less into each pocket, packing lightly. Dip stuffed chops into evaporated milk; roll in cracker crumbs. Brown in butter in skillet. Place in single layer in baking pan. Sprinkle a little seasoned pepper over chops. Cover; bake at 325 degrees 1 1/2 hours until tender. Remove chops to heated platter; garnish with parsley. Make a Milk Gravy to serve over chops. Serves 6.

Milk Gravy

2 tablespoons drippings

2 tablespoons flour   2 cups rich milk

1/2 teaspoon chicken bouillon   Salt and pepper to taste

Pour off all but 2 tablespoons grease in skillet; stir flour into drippings; let brown nicely before stirring in milk; lower heat; stir in milk. Continue to stir until gravy is creamy, smooth and thickened. Add seasonings to taste. More milk or less may be used, according to whether thick or thin gravy is desired.

Sweet Potato Stuffed Pork Steaks (Very special)

1 1/2 cups mashed sweet potato   I well-beaten egg

2 tablespoons corn syrup   6 thin pork steaks

Salt and pepper to taste   Cream of mushroom soup

1/8 teaspoon ginger   Onion powder

To the mashed sweet potato, add corn syrup, seasonings, and egg. Dip steaks in seasoned flour; spread each with 2 tablespoons of potato mixture. Roll; skewer with toothpicks. Place in greased shallow baking dish. Top each with a couple tablespoons of cream of mushroom soup; sprinkle tops with a little onion powder. Cover and bake in 350-degree oven until tender, about 1 hour. Uncover to brown. Serves 6.

Near Possum (A near cousin of Sweet Potato Stuffed Pork Steaks)

Fine cracker crumbs   6 thin slices pork steak or ham

Onion powder   1 1/2 cups mashed sweet potatoes

Evaporated milk   2 tablespoons brown sugar

Cream of mushroom soup   1 tablespoon butter

Salt and pepper to taste   1 well-beaten egg

Combine cooked, mashed, sweet potatoes, sugar, salt and pepper, butter, and well-beaten egg. Spoon about 2 tablespoons of mixture on each pork steak. Roll and skewer or tie. Roll in milk; coat with fine cracker crumbs; let set a few minutes. Brown in butter. Place in buttered baking dish. Top each roll with undiluted mushroom soup; sprinkle with onion powder. Cover and bake at 350 degrees

about 1 hour until tender, turning once during baking. Remove cover and brown. Serves 6.

Note: To make ahead, buy a leg of pork or ham—have butcher slice. Make and prepare "Near Possum." Roll and wrap each roll individually; freeze. Prepare as needed, first dipping in the milk, then cracker crumbs, then, spooning mushroom soup over and seasoning and baking.

Pork Cordon Bleu

4	pork cutlets	2	tablespoons flour
4	slices Swiss cheese		Salt and pepper to taste
4	thin slices cooked ham	1	cup evaporated milk
3	tablespoons butter		Dash of sage

Pound cutlets to 3/8-inch thick with meat mallet; place 1 slice each cheese and ham on each. Roll up, enclosing cheese and ham slices. Brown the rolls in heated butter in skillet; remove and reserve the drippings in skillet. Place rolls in baking dish. Bake at 325 degrees about 30 minutes until done.

Stir flour, salt, and dash of pepper into drippings. Cook and stir until smooth. Slowly add the milk; cook and stir until thickened and bubbly. Stir in sage. Serve over cutlets or in separate bowl. Serves 4.

Spareribs

Sweet 'n' Sour Spareribs

3	pounds lean spare ribs	2	tablespoons frozen orange
1 1/3	cups tomato juice	2	teaspoon soya sauce
2	teaspoons vinegar	2	teaspoons onion powder
2	tablespoons lemon juice		Salt and pepper to taste
4	tablespoons brown sugar	4	tablespoons pineapple juice
1	teaspoon Worcestershire sauce	4	slices pineapple diced
2	teaspoons cornstarch	2	tablespoons diced green pepper
1/2	teaspoon prepared mustard		

Place cut spareribs in roasting pan. Bake at 350 degrees for 1 1/4 hours. Bake at 450 degrees 10 minutes. Carefully drain off excess fat. While ribs are roasting, sauté diced green pepper in a tablespoon of butter in skillet; add all other ingredients (except cornstarch);

simmer together a few minutes. Taste to determine if you wish to add salt or other seasonings. Pour over spareribs. Cover and bake for another 45 or 50 minutes at 350 degrees. Remove spareribs. Pour off excess fat. Thicken with cornstarch (make a smooth paste with a little water) and add to simmering ingredients. Pour over spareribs. Serves 4.

Chinese Barbecued Spareribs

The spareribs you eat in many Chinese restaurants in this country are not necessarily what you would eat were you in China. Smoking of the ribs, most common in the Szechuan Province rarely is employed by American restaurants; the same is true of frying and steaming, the most common methods of preparing ribs in China. Most Chinese restaurants here use oven baking.

In general, Chinese spareribs taste the way they do because they are first marinated, and then cooked very slowly. The characteristic red color and distinctive flavor come from the use of hoisin sauce. It has a sweet, pungent taste and usually is available in cans and jars in the gourmet section of supermarkets and Asian markets.

(This recipe is similar to what you will get in most of the Chinese restaurants here.)

5 pounds pork ribs	2 quarter-size slices ginger root
1 clove garlic, mashed	shredded
1 tablespoon brown sugar	4 tablespoons hoisin sauce
1 tablespoon soy sauce	2 tablespoons rice wine or sherry

Cut ribs into individual pieces (or ask your butcher to cut the ribs into 2-inch lengths). Place ribs in single layer in a shallow pan. Combine remaining ingredients and pour over ribs. Let stand in refrigerator for at least 3 hours. Drain, reserving marinade.* Place ribs, curved side up, in baking pan; roast for 30 minutes in a 350 degree oven. Turn ribs over, baste with reserved marinade, and roast an additional 30 minutes.

*Do not eat the sauce unless you boil it first.

Ground Pork

Steamed Pork Dumplings

1/2 pound ground pork	12 mushrooms, finely chopped
1 egg, slightly beaten	2 scallions, finely chopped
1/2 teaspoon sugar	1 small stalk celery, finely
1 teaspoon soy sauce	chopped
Salt to taste	Dough Wrappers
1 tablespoon cornstarch	(recipe follows)

Combine the lean ground pork with all ingredients except the dough. Mix thoroughly and set aside.

On lightly floured surface, roll prepared dough to 1/8-inch thickness; cut into 3-inch circles. Place 1 tablespoon filling in center of each circle; bring sides of dough to cover the meat as much as possible without sealing completely; top of meat will be exposed. Place one layer of dumplings without touching each other on steamer rack over boiling water. Cover and steam dumplings for 30 minutes. Repeat with remaining dough, adding more water to steamer as necessary. Makes 20 dumplings.

Dough Wrappers

2 1/4 cups all-purpose flour	1 egg
1 egg yolk	1/2 teaspoon salt
1/2 cup water	1/2 teaspoon sugar

Sift together flour, sugar, and salt. In separate bowl beat together egg, egg yolk, and water. Make well in center of flour mixture; pour egg mixture into well. Mix together until a soft ball forms. Knead dough a few minutes until smooth but not stiff. Divide dough. Roll out on lightly floured surface and cut as desired. Makes 20.

Pork Stroganoff

1 pound ground lean pork	8 ounces mushrooms, chopped
1/2 cup cracker crumbs	1 small onion, chopped
1 egg, beaten	1 tablespoon flour
Salt and pepper to taste	1/2 cup broth or dry sherry
1 tablespoon butter	2/3 cup dairy sour cream

Combine pork, crumbs, egg, salt and pepper; shape into balls. Brown in butter in nonstick skillet; place balls on paper towel to drain. Cook onion and mushrooms in drippings in skillet until tender; stir in flour; stir in broth or sherry and 1/2 cup water; stir until smooth and thickened. Return meatballs and simmer 20 minutes. Remove from heat: stir in sour cream. Adjust seasonings. Serve over hot cooked noodles. Serves 4.

Hams

With the demands of a health-conscious society, ham is as much as 57 percent leaner than the ham of 20 years ago.

A 3-ounce serving of ham has less cholesterol than a 3-ounce skinless chicken breast, the same amount of calories, and somewhat higher fat content.

However, be aware of the high sodium content in most ham products, because sodium compounds are added in the curing process.

Numerous specialty hams are on the market, a result of different curing methods. Perhaps the best known is country or country-style ham, such as Smithfield®. Country hams are slowly dry-cured with salt, then smoked and aged.

Styles of Ham

Boneless hams: All bones have been removed and most of the fat trimmed away before being fully cooked. Processors section the ham, remove the fat and bone and reform the ham.

Canned hams: Boneless, placed in cans, vacuum-sealed and then fully cooked. Natural dry gelatin may be added before sealing to absorb the juices as the ham cooks.

Bone-in hams: Sold in whole hams, shank and rump halves, shank and rump portions, and center slices. Some hams are semiboneless with only the round-leg bone or the shank bone remaining.

A boneless or canned ham will yield four to five servings per pound, while a bone-in ham gives you two to three servings per pound.

Pre-cooked hams are in three categories: Cook-before-eating, ready-to-eat, and fully cooked. All three have been heated, in compliance with government regulations, to an internal temperature of 137 degrees or more. This temperature is adequate to destroy any harmful bacteria.

To Bake A Whole Ham

If directions for baking come with the ham, follow them exactly. Otherwise bake as follows: Place ham, fat side up on rack in shallow, open, roasting pan. Insert thermometer into center of thickest part of ham without letting the bulb touch the bone or rest in fat. For fully cooked hams, roast at 325 degrees to an internal temperature of 140 degrees; for a cook-before-eating ham, roast to a temperature of 160 degrees.

Favorite Ham Loaf

3/4	pound lean ground ham	1	egg, beaten
3/4	pound lean ground pork	1/2	cup milk
3/4	cup cracker crumbs	1/4	cup brown sugar
1	teaspoon parsley flakes	1	teaspoon prepared mustard
1/8	teaspoon pepper	1	tablespoon vinegar

Combine ham, pork, cracker crumbs, parsley flakes and pepper. Place in 9- by 5-inch buttered loaf pan. Bake at 350 degrees 30 minutes. Top with blended sugar, mustard, and vinegar and bake another hour. Serve on hot platter; garnish with sautéed apple or pineapple slices. Serves 4 to 6.

Breakfast, Lunch, and Supper Treats (Using leftover ham)

Ham Scramble: Slightly butter nonstick skillet with butter; heat ham cubes or slivers until lightly browned; pour in scrambled-egg mixture and scramble as usual. If you like, top mixture with shredded cheddar cheese.

Ham Benedict: Split and toast one English muffin for each serving. Top each muffin half with thinly sliced or slivered ham; add a slice of broiled tomato. On top of this place a poached egg, then a generous spoonful of heated cheese sauce (your favorite cheese sauce, or even a pasteurized process cheese spread).

Macaroni, Cheese, and Ham: Add diced ham to your favorite macaroni-and-cheese mixture before baking.

And use those last little bits: to top hot cooked vegetables; to add to macaroni, egg, chicken, or shrimp salad, or cottage cheese; to sprinkle over cream soups; to grind and mix with cream cheese for a dip or sandwich spread; to mix with sour cream topping for baked potato.

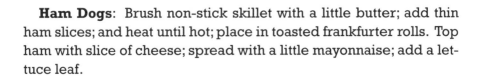

Ham Dogs: Brush non-stick skillet with a little butter; add thin ham slices; and heat until hot; place in toasted frankfurter rolls. Top ham with slice of cheese; spread with a little mayonnaise; add a lettuce leaf.

Ham Soufflé

2 eggs, separated	1 cup milk, scalded
1 teaspoon onion powder	3/4 cup Ritz® cracker crumbs
1/4 teaspoon mustard	3/4 cup cooked ground ham
1/8 teaspoon pepper	1 tablespoon minced parsley

Combine ground leftover ham (or Spam®), cracker crumbs, and seasonings; stir into scalded milk. Beat egg whites. In another container, without washing beater, beat egg yolks, and stir yolks into ham mixture. Fold in beaten egg whites. Pour into unbuttered oven-proof baking dish. Bake at 325 degrees until golden brown—about 45 minutes. Serves 4.

Bacon

Bacon should have a good proportion of lean meat and be properly cured. It cannot take much heat. Place in a cold pan to bake, broil, or fry to keep it from curling.

Sautéed Bacon

Place strips of bacon in cold pan. Sauté slowly, turning frequently; keep pouring off accumulated grease. Watch carefully; bacon burns in seconds, and old bacon burns twice as fast as fresh. Place sautéed bacon between absorbent paper towels to drain off fat.

Broiled bacon

Preheat broiler. Place bacon strips on broiler rack over drip pan. Broil about 5 inches from source of heat; broil until golden and crisp. Drain on absorbent paper towels.

Bacon in the Oven

When preparing a quantity of bacon for a large gathering for a breakfast brunch, lunch, or dinner, do it in the oven. Separate bacon slices and arrange slices on rack in a broiler pan or large shallow

baking pan. Bake at 400 degrees about 12 minutes until slightly browned and crisp. (To prevent spattering, add a little water to boiler pan under bacon rack.) No need to turn bacon as it does not curl as much as pan fried. Or set oven at 375 degrees and allow a little longer time to bake. Transfer slices to paper towels to absorb grease.

Canadian Bacon

Canadian Bacon is not bacon at all but one of the most expensive cuts of pork—the loin. In other words, it is the very heart of the pork chop. It is made from this delicacy of loin, trimmed of all but a few strips of fat, then cured and smoked. It would be more appropriate to call it "Smoked Loin of Pork." It doesn't taste like bacon, being less salty and having very little fat.

Sliced and slowly browned on both sides, it is delicious. Slice about 1/4-inch thick. Place in buttered skillet; cook over low heat 3 to 5 minutes, turning frequently, until lightly browned on each side.

What is beef bacon?

Since Government regulations forbid its being called "bacon," it is packaged as "breakfast beef." It is available in 1/2-pound packages (12 to 14 slices).

Crumbled Prepared Bacon

Prepared bacon, crumbled, adds flavor and interest to various dishes:
  - Add to muffin batter just before pouring into baking cups.
  - Add to waffle batter just before baking.
  - Toss with crisp salad greens; dress with oil and vinegar.
  - Use as seasoner for fresh-cooked green vegetables such as peas, beans, chopped spinach.
  - Use as topping for macaroni and cheese casserole.
  - Stir into peanut butter or egg salad for sandwich filling.
  - Use as topping for scrambled eggs.
  - Top servings of spaghetti and meat sauce.
  - Add to heated pork and beans just before serving.
  - Sprinkle over hot baked potatoes, right on top of the melted butter or dairy sour cream.

Blanching Bacon

Bacon strips should be blanched before wrapping them around a roast. Bacon is wrapped around a roast to prevent it from drying out during cooking. As the bacon fat melts in the oven, it automatically bastes the meat. Cooking the bacon briefly in simmering water accomplishes several things. It removes some of the smoky flavor that might otherwise overpower the flavor of the roast, it eliminates some of the salt, and it keeps the bacon from becoming too crisp too quickly, enabling it to perform its moisturizing task more effectively.

Veal

Americans have had plenty of room and plenty of cheap grass and grain, so they grew their calves into steers and ate beef. In Europe it has long been cheaper to make calves into veal as soon as they were weaned from the cow. True milk-fed veal is delicious.

Veal is meat of young calves, generally about six weeks old. Except for the very thin cuts, cook veal at a low temperature, using a moist-heat method to keep veal tender and retain the delicate flavor. Since veal is young and lacks fat and connective tissues, veal requires careful cooking. Very thin cuts should be cooked in butter. Larger cuts, after the initial browning, are covered and baked slowly until fork tender.

Pan-frying is the most popular method of preparing veal scallops, cutlets, and chops. Because of the thinness of the cut, the veal will cook through before it has time to lose its moistness or becomes less tender.

Although veal is limited in supply, and therefore relatively expensive per pound, there is almost no waste in most retail cuts.

Veal Cutlets Special

4 veal cutlets (4-ounce each)	1/4 teaspoon chicken bouillon
4 slices Swiss cheese	Salt and pepper to taste
4 slices ham (1-ounce each)	Ritz® cracker crumbs
1 egg, slightly beaten	1 tablespoon cream

Pound veal cutlets very thin. On one half of each cutlet, place a slice of Swiss cheese and a slice of ham; fold over the side of cutlet to cover. Pound edges together to seal. Season with salt, pepper, and chicken bouillon. Beat egg and cream together; dip veal in egg mixture; roll in fine cracker crumbs. Let set in refrigerator about 20 minutes. Pan fry in clarified butter about 20 minutes. Serve Gravy Cream Sauce (recipe follows) on the side. Serves 4.

Gravy Cream Sauce

1 teaspoon onion powder	3-ounce can sliced mushrooms
1/4 teaspoon paprika	1/2 cup dry wine (or broth)
1 cup sour cream	Salt and pepper to taste
1 tablespoon flour	

Sauté mushrooms seasoned with onion powder, salt and pepper in skillet where cutlets were sautéed; add wine and paprika; bring to a rolling boil, scraping up browned bits from pan. Stir tablespoon of flour into mixture; simmer until hot and slightly thickened. Adjust seasonings. Either pour over cutlets and serve at once, or serve in bowl for each person to pour over cutlet as desired.

Beef

There are two basic types of meat: tough and tender. (Tender cuts such as rib, tenderloin, and sirloin are from the section of the animal that is rarely used in movement and has little connective tissue. Cuts such as chuck, brisket, and round, found in the leg area of the animal, contain frequently used muscles and more connective tissue and are therefore less tender.) There is a basic cooking method for each: dry heat for tender meat; moist heat for tough meat.

Various dry heat methods of cooking include broiling, pan-broiling, frying, and roasting. There are thousands of recipes for various cuts of meat under each heading. But one thing these methods have in common is the fact that they use no moisteners, and therefore, have little or no tenderizing effect on the meat. In fact, dry cooking, if overdone, tends to toughen. Heat solidifies the protein in meat, and once you get past the medium rare you have some pretty solid protein that gets increasingly harder to chew as it becomes overdone.

Moist heat contributes to the tenderness of meat. Long slow cooking in liquid breaks down the connective tissue and turns it into gelatin. Moist-heat methods of cooking include stewing, simmering, braising, or cooking in liquid. And for every thousand recipes for dry heat cooking, there will likely be a million for moist heat—that is because there is a lot more tough meat in the world than there is tender.

Keep in mind that much of the flavor of the meat has drained out of the meat into the pan in the moist-heat process. To get the flavor back requires making a sauce; but don't worry, most sauces are little more than what's left in the pan after you've cooked something with moist heat—mixed with a little imagination. With experience you'll find any cut of meat cooked right need not be tough.

Selecting the Meat: Knowing the Cuts

Knowing both the meat cuts and how much to buy are valuable factors in making meat selection easy.

Boneless: Allow 1/4 to 1/3 pound per serving (ground meat, meats for stews and soups, boneless roasts and steaks).

Bone-in-meat: Allow 1/3 to 1/2 pound per serving (roasts and steaks with moderate amount of bone).

Bony Meat: Allow 3/4 to 1 pound per serving. Note: 3 ounces of cooked meat is considered a serving, but more than one serving may be desired by some people.

Tender Steaks: T-bone, Rib (Rib Eye), Tenderloin (Filet Mignon), Sirloin (Top Sirloin), Club, and Porterhouse are best broiled or barbecued.

Less Tender Steaks: Round Steak, Chuck, and Blade, unless tenderized, are best braised.

Oven Roast: Standing Rib, Rib Eye, Rolled Rib, Tenderloin, Rump, Rolled Round, and Sirloin Tip should be cooked without liquid.

Pot Roast: Blade Bone Roast (Chuck), Arm Bone Roast (Chuck), Boneless Chuck Pot Roast, Beef Brisket, Corned Beef ("Corned" refers to a curing process) need to be cooked with liquid. Heel of Round (less tender than rump) should be cooked with liquid unless it has been tenderized.

Steaks

Steak is enjoyed internationally; it is the most popular dinner item on American restaurant menus. And according to the *Encyclopedia Britannica*, beef contains the highest form of protein for human consumption, in the most palatable, stimulating, and digestible form.

There are many theories on how best to cook a steak, and if you have found the perfect way, stick to it.

To help you determine if your steak is rare, medium, or any other way you want it, use the timing technique for a 1 1/4 inch steak. Bring steaks to room temperature. First sear the steak on both sides; then cook 3 minutes on each side for very rare; 4 minutes for rare; 5 minutes for medium rare; 6 minutes for medium. If steak is more than 1 1/4-inches thick, lengthen the time slightly. But keep in mind a "well done" steak is not as tender as a rare one.

As for seasoning, salt and pepper the steak after it has been turned; or salt and pepper just before serving; or let each person season according to personal preference when served.

Basic Pan-Broiled Steak

1 to 4 steaks cut 1-inch thick or less

1 to 2 tablespoons Clarified Butter*, or more

Salt and seasoned pepper

In heavy skillet over medium-high heat, melt butter; sear steaks (not touching each other) well on both sides, turning with tongs; do not pierce with fork. Reduce heat to medium and continue cooking, turning often, until degree of doneness desired. Sprinkle with salt and pepper to taste.

Cooking time is usually shorter than in broiling. A 1-inch thick steak will take approximately 3 to 4 minutes on each side for medium rare.

* Clarified Butter is butter with milk solids removed. The clear yellow liquid that remains can be heated to a high temperature without burning.

To clarify butter: Melt 1/2 cup butter in a small pan or heatproof glass container over low heat or in microwave. Do not boil. Skim foam from the surface (save in small jar to use to flavor vegetables). Then carefully tip container and pour the clear part of butter into a container, leaving the milky residue behind. (Dispose of milky residue.)

Oven-Broiled Steaks

Tender steaks, cut at least 1 1/2-inches thick

Set rack 4 inches from heat source and preheat broiler. Place steak on rack on broiler pan and broil until browned, about 3 minutes per side. Turn oven to 375 degrees and continue cooking steaks, turning often, until desired doneness is reached. Season with salt and pepper; serve on heated platter.

Grilled Sirloin Steak

1 3-pound sirloin steak, cut 2 inches thick

Salt and pepper to taste

Place steak on rack in shallow baking pan. Roast at 400 degrees 10 to 12 minutes per side for rare, 12 to 15 minutes per side for medium rare, and 15 to 18 minutes per side for well done. (For best results, use a meat thermometer and undercook a few degrees.) Turn only once. Season to taste with salt and pepper after turning. When steak is done, remove from heat and place in warm spot for about 10 minutes to let juices set. To serve, carve across grain in thin slices, allowing 2 to 3 slices per person.

Steak or a Roast?

The distinction between a steak and a roast isn't precise. A slice cut from a rib section would probably be called a steak; but a thicker cut from the same section that would require a different method of cooking would be called a roast.

Beef Roasts

To Roast Standing Ribs of Beef

Heat oven to 325 degrees. Place roast, fat side up, in shallow, open roasting pan. Season with salt and pepper, if desired. Insert meat thermometer so tip comes to center part of roast without touching bone or resting in fat. Roast until thermometer registers 140 degrees for rare (allow 18 to 20 minutes per pound), 160 degrees for medium (22 to 25 minutes per pound), 170 degrees for well done (27 to 30 minutes per pound). Remove roast to heated platter. Let rest 10 to 15 minutes. This lets meat firm up, makes carving easier, and retains the juices.

Beef Roasts	Weight (pounds)	Internal temp when removed from oven	Total Cooking Time (hours)
Standing Rib	4 to 6	140° (rare)	2 1/4 to 2 3/4
		160° (medium)	2 3/4 to 3 1/4
		170° (well done)	3 1/4 to 3 1/2
Standing Rib	6 to 8	140° (rare)	2 3/4 to 3
		160° (medium)	3 to 3 1/2
		170° (well done)	3 1/4 to 4
Rolled Rib	5 to 7	140° (rare)	3 1/4 to 3 1/2
		160° (medium)	3 3/4 to 4
		170° (well done)	4 1/2 to 4 3/4
Rolled Rump	4 to 6	150° to 170°	2 to 2 1/2
Sirloin Tip	3 to 4	150° to 170°	2 to 2 3/4
Rib Eye or	4 to 6	140° (rare)	1 1/2 to 1 3/4
Delmonico (350°)		160° (medium)	1 3/4
		170° (well done)	2
Tenderloin (425°)	4 to 6	140° (rare)	45 min. to I hr.

Pot Roast
Moist-Heat Method

Pot roast is a popular term applied to braising large cuts. The cooking may be done on top of the range or in a low temperature oven (300 to 325 degrees).

Brown meat in a small amount of fat and cook slowly in a covered utensil; the natural meat juices are allowed to collect or a small amount of liquid is added. A tight-fitting lid should be used to hold in the steam needed for softening the connective tissue and tenderizing the meat. Cooking is done at a low temperature until meat is tender. This means simmering, not boiling. A sauce or gravy may be made from the liquid in the pan and is a desirable part of many braised meat dishes.

Stewing or Cooking in Liquid

Large, less tender cuts and stew meat are simmered in liquid in a covered utensil. The meat should be covered with water or stock. The liquid may be hot or cold to start. By entirely covering the meat with liquid, uniform cooking is assured without turning the meat. Do not boil the meat. Boiling shrinks the meat and makes it dry, difficult to slice, and detracts from flavor and texture. Meat is fully cooked when it is fork-tender. Wisely used seasonings add much to the variety and flavor of meats that are cooked in liquid. Some suggestions are: bay leaves, thyme, marjoram, parsley, green pepper, celery and onion tops, garlic, cloves, peppercorns, and allspice.

Brown–in–Bag Pot Roast with Vegetables

6 small potatoes	1 3 or 4-pound beef pot roast
6 carrots, pared	1 envelope dry onion soup mix
Flour	1/3 cup water

Trim excess fat from meat. Rub roast with flour. Place bag in pan and sprinkle half of onion soup mix on bottom inside bag; place roast in bag and arrange vegetables around roast. Sprinkle remaining onion soup mix over entire surface of roast and vegetables; add water. Tie-bag and puncture 6 small holes in top. Cook in 325-degree oven 2 to 2 1/2 hours. Pierce with fork to test for doneness. The bag holds natural juices in and around meat; makes the meat baste itself, moist and tender.

Ground Beef

The United States Department of Agriculture recommends that ground beef always be cooked to 160 degrees, which is substantially higher than the 145 degrees (medium rare, pink inside) that is recommended for beef steaks, chops, and roasts (including lamb roasts).

While bacteria may be present on all meat, they generally remain on the surface of whole cuts and are easily destroyed during cooking. Ground meat is more risky. Extra handling makes it particularly susceptible to contamination, and the grinding process distributes the bacteria throughout the meat, making thorough cooking essential.

Talk of the Town Steaks

4 slices bacon	1 1/2 pounds ground top round
1/4 cup evaporated milk	1/2 teaspoon chicken bouillon
Salt and pepper to taste	

Sprinkle chicken bouillon, milk, salt, and pepper over meat; blend. Form into 4 patties 1-inch thick. Wrap each with bacon slice and secure with toothpicks. Broil to desired doneness.

Broiled Surprise Patties

Shape 'Talk of the Town Steak" mixture into 8 flat patties. Place on center of each of 4 patties a slice of cheese 2-inches square. Cover each with a second patty; seal edges. Place a strip of bacon around edge, holding together with a toothpick. Place patties on broiler rack. Broil slowly 10 minutes on each side about 4 inches from heat.

Potato Burgers

1 1/2 cups grated potato	1 1/2 pounds lean ground beef
1/2 teaspoon salt	1/4 teaspoon seasoned pepper
1/4 cup evaporated milk	1 teaspoon onion powder

Peel and grate 2 medium potatoes into a bowl of cold water, rinse, drain, and dry on paper towels. Add milk and seasonings to ground beef; blend in grated potatoes. Shape into patties; cook in slightly buttered nonstick skillet until crusty and cooked through on each side. These should not be rare. Serve hot on toasted bun.

What is Hamburger?

According to United States Department of Agriculture, the only difference between "hamburger" and "ground beef" is the optional addition of a bit of extra fat. But no one adds fat to make it a "hamburger" anymore.

Most meat markets make their ground beef from the trimmings that are a natural part of the meat-cutting process. When a butcher trims the tail off a T-bone steak, or "squares up" a rolled roast, the trimmings go into ground beef. The less tender portions of the beef—the plate and shank and brisket, those cuts that just will not sell—are trimmed of their excess fat and ground. From those trimmings we get ground beef.

For the lowest fat content, have a beef bottom round roast or a lean chuck arm roast trimmed of fat and ground to order.

Hamburger

The leaner the meat, the better the hamburger. Handle the ground meat as little and as lightly as possible. The less "fixing" it gets, the juicier and more tender it will be. When shaping into patties, pat the meat gently and evenly into rounds or squares—as thick at the edges as at the center—so they will cook evenly throughout. Learn by experimenting a bit on your own how a little club soda, water, milk, tomato juice, or broth added to a hamburger mixture just before you shape it into patties helps to make the hamburgers extra tender, light, and juicy. Try adding a little grated potato (rinsed in cold water, drained and dried), a little cream or evaporated milk, seasoned pepper, onion powder, and salt to the ground meat—really delicious and moist.

Broil or fry your hamburger the way you find most desirable for yourself. If you brown your meat quickly on either side, cover it; then turn heat to lower and finish to correct doneness for your taste, turning a couple times, you will have a juicy burger.

Garnish the burger with cheese (melted on the bun, not on the meat) and add lettuce, tomato, and mayonnaise.

Zucchini Meat Loaf

2/3 cup Bisquick® baking mix	1 tablespoon chopped green
1 egg	bell pepper
3/4 cup shredded zucchini	1/2 teaspoon seasoned salt
1/4 cup shredded carrots	Pepper to taste
1/2 pound lean ground beef	1/4 teaspoon Knorr® seasoning

Beat egg and mix with Bisquick® and zucchini until well blended. Mix in remaining ingredients. Shape into patty, about 7 inches in diameter, in a lightly buttered pie plate. Bake in a 375-degree oven about 30 minutes, covered the last 10 minutes of baking. Should be brown when done. Serves 4.

Ad Lib Hash

Vary recipe according to what you have on hand. Combine equal parts finely diced or chopped cooked potatoes and cooked meat in a bowl. Season as desired with onion powder, salt, and seasoned pepper. Add enough milk, cream, or meat gravy to moisten. Press into buttered skillet; heat through and turn. Top each serving with a poached egg. Four cups mixture will serve 4 people.

Meat Rollups

Favorite biscuit dough	2 tablespoons chopped onion
2 cups ground cooked meat	Salt and pepper to taste
2 tablespoons sour cream	1 teaspoon prepared mustard

Roll biscuit dough 1/4-inch thick and about 9- by 15-inches. Spread with ground cooked meat combined with other ingredients. Roll as for jelly roll; cut in 1-inch slices. Place on lightly buttered cookie sheet. Bake at 425 degrees 12 to 15 minutes. Serve with gravy.

Creamed Chipped Beef on Toast

1/4 cup butter	2 2.5-ounce packages of
1/4 cup flour	thin-sliced beef or pastrami
2 cups milk	cut into small squares
4 toast slices	

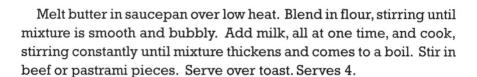

Melt butter in saucepan over low heat. Blend in flour, stirring until mixture is smooth and bubbly. Add milk, all at one time, and cook, stirring constantly until mixture thickens and comes to a boil. Stir in beef or pastrami pieces. Serve over toast. Serves 4.

Family Meat Loaf

1 teaspoon butter	1 teaspoon Worcestershire
1/4 cup chopped onion	sauce
1 pound lean ground beef	1/4 cup ketchup
1 large egg	1/2 teaspoon salt
1 cup bread crumbs	1/8 teaspoon pepper

Heat oven to 350 degrees. Heat butter in a small frying pan over medium heat: add chopped onion and cook until onion is tender, about 5 minutes. Remove from heat and cool.

Combine remaining ingredients in a large bowl; mix well. Stir in onion. Stir mixture into an 8x4-inch loaf pan. Bake 45 to 50 minutes or until meat thermometer inserted in center registers 160 degrees. Let cool a few minutes before removing from pan. Makes 4 servings.

Meat Loaf Supreme

1 pound ground lean beef	1 cup Ritz® cracker crumbs
I pound ground lean pork	1/8 teaspoon pepper
1 cup shredded carrots	1 egg, slightly beaten
1/4 cup minced onions	1/2 teaspoon salt
1 cup sour cream	2 teaspoons minced parsley
1/2 cup minced celery	1/4 teaspoon thyme

Combine meats, carrots, celery, onions, salt, and pepper. In small bowl combine egg, sour cream, and cracker crumbs; blend the two mixtures together; pack into 9x5x3-inch loaf pan. At this point, spread top with mixture of 2 tablespoons ketchup and 1 teaspoon brown sugar. Bake at 350 degrees until loaf barely pulls from sides of pan, about 1 1/4 to 1 1/2 hours. Makes 4 to 6 servings.

Potato-Beef Bake

    4 cups sliced potatoes

    1 cup grated processed American cheese

    1 teaspoon dried parsley flakes

    1 1/2 ounce envelope onion soup mix

    1 pound lean ground beef

1 2/3 cup evaporated milk

    1/2 cup Ritz® cracker crumbs

Toss together potatoes, cheese, and parsley flakes. Spread in bottom of buttered 2-quart casserole. Sprinkle 1/2 of onion soup mix over top.

Mix together ground beef, evaporated milk, cracker crumbs, and remaining onion soup mix. Spread mixture over potatoes. Cover. Bake in a 350-degree oven until beef is well browned and cooked through, about 1 hour. Let set a few minutes; loosen edges by running a knife around edge; loosen bottom with spatula; place serving plate top down over casserole; holding platter, quickly turn over so potatoes are on top. Serve hot. Serves 6.

Soufflé Ground Beef Pie

        9-inch pie shell with high fluted edge

    1 teaspoon butter

    2 medium onions, minced

1 1/2 pounds extra lean beef, ground

    1/2 cup water

    1 egg beaten

    1 tablespoon flour

    2 tablespoons snipped parsley

    1/6 teaspoon thyme

        Salt and pepper to taste

Sauté minced onions in the teaspoon of butter in heated nonstick skillet; add lean ground beef; cook until browned. Add water; bring to boil; remove from heat.

Combine beaten egg, flour, parsley and seasonings: stir into beef

mixture. Spoon mixture into pie shell. Bake on bottom shelf in a 425-degree oven for 15 minutes; remove and reduce oven temperature to 375 degrees.

Meanwhile prepare the Cheese Souffle mixture; spread it over beef mixture. In pie shell, sealing to edges of shell all around. Bake at 375 degrees until golden brown. Serve immediately. Serves 4 to 6.

Cheese Souffle

2 tablespoons butter	1 cup shredded Cheddar cheese
2 tablespoons flour	2 egg yolks
1/2 cup milk	2 egg whites, room temperature

Melt butter in nonstick saucepan; stir in flour; then the milk. Cook over medium heat, stirring until thickened. Stir in cheese until smooth; remove from heat. Stir in slightly beaten egg yolks. Beat egg whites until stiff peaks form; fold into cheese mixture.

Pie Crust

1 1/2 cups sifted flour	3 tablespoons ice water
Pinch of salt	1 1/2 teaspoons vinegar
5/8 cup Crisco®	1 egg yolk

With blending fork, work the Crisco into sifted dry ingredients. Beat together vinegar, egg, and water; blend into flour mixture. Pastry dough will keep for several days in an airtight container in refrigerator. Use as needed. Very easy to roll. Double recipe If desired, using a whole egg.

Vegetables

With such a variety of fresh vegetables on the market—as well as frozen and canned—and with so many ways of serving them attractively (such as, arranging two or more on a platter or chop plate, arranging them around meat, or a vegetable dinner on individual plates), each meal should be an interesting, delicious experience. It is important to have a variety of vegetables, and the aim should be to cook them with care and serve them attractively.

Steam cooking is a method of cooking that preserves the natural flavor and nutrients of fresh vegetables. You can turn almost any saucepan into a vegetable steamer if you have a self adjusting stainless steel basket (don't use aluminum). To steam vegetables, place uniform-size pieces in the steamer basket. The basket prevents the vegetables from coming in contact with the water. In a saucepan bring water to boiling. Place the basket of vegetables over the boiling water, making sure the water does not touch the basket. Cover saucepan; reduce heat after the steaming process starts. During cooking, test vegetables as little as possible so steam will not escape. Steam until crisp-tender. Check the water level, refilling with boiling water if necessary. Steaming takes longer than some other methods, but the results are very desirable.

Steamed Mixed Vegetables

Use amounts and variety of vegetables desired. Cut all the vegetables in as near uniform size as possible. Just remember the bottom layer in the steamer cooks faster. Chicken bouillon is a great booster of vegetable flavor and may be added when vegetables are put into the steamer. Add salt and pepper or any other seasonings later. The following combination will serve 4.

    2 medium carrots, scraped and sliced diagonally

    1 cup cauliflower flowerets

    2 small zucchini, unpeeled and sliced

    2 stalks celery, scraped and sliced diagonally

    2 stalks broccoli, peeled and sliced diagonally

    2 small yellow squash, unpeeled and sliced

6-ounce package frozen Chinese pea pods, optional

Chicken bouillon

Onion powder, salt, pepper, and sugar to suit taste

Melted butter to pour over vegetables when serving

Place vegetables in steamer basket in order listed. Cover and steam over simmering water about 12 minutes until crispy-tender. Season; arrange on heated platter; pour melted butter over top to serve. Garnish with sprig of parsley.

Artichokes

Globe Artichokes

The globe artichoke, with a head of clustered overlapping fleshy leaves, is the edible flower head of a tall thistle-like plant. It has a hairy center called the choke, and below that is the heart (called the fond). The globe artichoke is cooked like a vegetable; both the base of the leaves and the heart are edible; the choke is discarded. It contains more protein than most vegetables and a form of starch that is not readily utilized by the body, which makes it excellent for a restricted or low-calorie diet. It is high in potassium, phosphorus, and vitamins A and D. There is no other vegetable that can compare with its nut-like flavor.

You will often hear off-the-cuff remarks when this artichoke is served, such as:

Eating an artichoke is rather like consulting a daisy: "He loves me, he loves me not" pulling off the petals one by one.

Or, "One thing about an artichoke? It enables you to turn over a new leaf."

Or, "Of all the vegetables on earth
 It is quite the queerest one no doubt
 You have more when you are through with it
 Then when you started out."

To Prepare for Cooking

Thoroughly wash artichoke; cut stem off flush with the base; trim off lowest outer petals and cut off about 1 inch of top of artichoke. Then proceed to cook either the conventional way or in the microwave.

Conventional Cooking Method

Do not use an iron or aluminum pan. Bring water to a boil in a stainless steel, glass, enamel or nonstick container. Add 1/4 teaspoon salt for each artichoke and 1 tablespoon lemon juice or vinegar. Plunge the prepared artichoke upright into the boiling water. Cover and boil 20 to 45 minutes, depending on size of artichoke, until a leaf can easily be removed. Do not overcook. Drain upside down.

To Microwave Artichokes

The microwave makes quick work of 1, 2, 3, or 4 artichokes; but for more that 4, use conventional cooking. The microwave is ideal for cooking an artichoke for one person.

For cooking one artichoke:

1 large artichoke	1 tablespoon lemon juice
1/3 cup water	1 tablespoon oil

Any salad oil may be used but Bertolli Lucca® Extra Light™ Olive Oil is ideal. Place artichoke stem-side up in microwave safe glass measuring cup large enough to hold it. Add water, lemon juice, and oil. Cover with plastic wrap and microwave on HIGH 7 to 10 minutes. Give container half-turn halfway through cooking time. Remove from oven and immediately turn right side up in liquid; cover and let stand 5 minutes. Drain and serve on salad plate.

For cooking four large artichokes:

4 large artichokes	4 slices lemon
1/4 cup water	1 tablespoon oil

Place prepared artichokes stem-side up in small microwave-proof casserole just large enough to hold them; add remaining ingredients. Microwave, covered, on HIGH for 16 minutes. Remove from oven and immediately turn right side up in liquid. Let stand, covered, 5 minutes. Drain and serve.

To Serve Artichokes

Place cooked artichokes upright on individual salad plates so waste leaves will not clutter dinner plates. Pour melted butter into

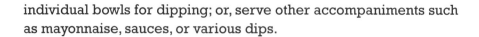

individual bowls for dipping; or, serve other accompaniments such as mayonnaise, sauces, or various dips.

To Eat Artichokes

Pull off leaves one by one and dip the base in desired accompaniments. Eat only the tender base of leaf by drawing it between teeth, discarding the remaining leaf. Continue eating until you reach the fuzz in center (or choke). Remove fuzz with a spoon; discard. This exposes the heart or the choicest part. Cut into bite size pieces, dip, and eat.

To Stuff Artichokes

After cooked artichoke has been drained, spread leaves apart gently; pull out center; scrape out fuzz with small spoon; stuff with any desired filling.

Artichoke Benedict Special

4 medium-size artichokes	4 eggs
4 1/4-inch thick slices	Cheese Sauce
baked ham, grated	

Wash artichokes. Cut off stems at base and remove small bottom leaves and cut off about 1-inch of top.

Stand artichokes upright in deep saucepan large enough to hold snugly. Add a teaspoon of salt and tablespoon of vinegar to 2-3 inches boiling water. Cover and boil gently 35 to 45 minutes or until base can be easily pierced with a fork. (Add a little more boiling water if needed.) Turn artichokes upside down to drain.

Spread leaves open like flower petals. Carefully remove center petals and fuzzy centers from artichoke bottoms with a spoon and discard; keep artichokes warm.

Prepare the eggs: In small container, mix 1/4 cup evaporated milk with desired seasoning (such as Knorr® seasoning, chicken bouillon, onion powder, salt, or pepper). Divide into 4 buttered, 5-ounce custard cups; top each with an egg. Set cups on rack in skillet with hot water coming almost to bottom of cups. Cover and steam over simmering water until yolks set.

While eggs are poaching prepare sauce:

Cheese Sauce

1 tablespoon butter	1/2 cup shredded Cheddar cheese
1 tablespoon flour	Salt and pepper to taste
1 cup milk	1/4 teaspoon onion powder

Melt butter; stir in flour; blend in seasonings. Gradually stir in milk. Cook, stirring, over medium heat until mixture boils and thickens. Stir in cheese until barely melted.

Place prepared artichokes on individual salad plates. Spread a little of the grated ham in center of each; stir remainder grated ham into sauce. Spread about a teaspoon of sauce over top. Then turn poached egg, upside down, over top and cover with remaining sauce. Serve immediately.

Asparagus

Asparagus is a good source of vitamins A and C, potassium and dietary fibers, and it is low in sodium. Depending on size, four spears contain only about 15 calories.

Select straight, firm stalks with closed, compact tips. One pound of asparagus yields about 1/2 to 3/4 pound trimmed, about 3 servings. (The diameter of the stalks is not related to tenderness of asparagus.)

To prepare, break off asparagus spears as far down as they snap easily. Brittle spears break, separating tender upper ends from woody base. Discard ends. Wash thoroughly. Then cook according to your favorite method.

For the true asparagus devotee, butter and salt are enough adornment. Some like to add lemon juice with the seasonings; some like to add a little cream; others prefer sauces such as cheese or Hollandaise.

Steaming Asparagus

Place washed, trimmed, fresh asparagus in a single layer on a rack over boiling water in a large skillet. Cover and steam to desired doneness (8 to 15 minutes). Test with your fingers for desired texture. Serve with melted butter and salt.

Another excellent method is to stand trimmed stalks, heads up, in a very tall coffee pot or other tall pot and add 2 or 3 inches boiling

water. Cover and steam. This allows bottoms to boil while more tender upper parts steam.

Choice Asparagus

Place single layer of prepared fresh asparagus spears flat in a large shallow skillet; cover with 1/2-inch cold water, 1/2 teaspoon salt and 1/2 teaspoon sugar. Boil 5 minutes. Let stand, uncovered, 5 minutes or until ready to serve. Drain; serve with melted butter. Cooked by this method, asparagus is never limp, overcooked, or grayed.

Asparagus Benedict

On a buttered, toasted half of an English muffin, place one thin slice sauteed chicken breast or ham and three tender-crisp cooked asparagus spears. Top with a poached egg and warm cheese or Hollandaise sauce, or a cream sauce. Garnish with a sprig of parsley.

A Favorite Salad

1 can asparagus	4 red sweet pepper rings
2 ripe tomatoes	4 green sweet pepper rings
2 hard-cooked eggs	Miracle Whip® salad dressing
4 stuffed olives	Onion powder, sugar to taste
Watercress	

Border chilled salad plates with watercress. Top with thin tomato slices around plate, sprinkled lightly with sugar and onion powder. Lay asparagus spears across center; add egg slices either side of asparagus spears. Top with tablespoon dressing and place stuffed olive in center. Cross pepper rings over top. Serves 4.

Green Beans

String and Snap Beans

Years ago they were called string beans. But with a real effort to breed the string out of string beans, we now identify them as snap beans. To prepare, they no longer have strings to remove; just snip off tips at either end before cooking.

Select green beans that are slender and smooth with no blemishes or brown spots. The pod should be pliant, but firm enough to snap easily when bent, best when the tiny beans within haven't even begun to bulge. (The bigger the bulge, the tougher the pod—they've lost their snap by then. Bulging pods indicate overmaturity.)

Green beans are an excellent source of vitamins A, B_1, and C. They also provide quite a bit of iron and calcium.

Purchase about 1/4 pound per person and store the unwashed beans in a plastic bag in refrigerator 3 to 5 days until ready to prepare. Or purchase the frozen young green beans and store in freezer.

Quick Cooked Green Beans

2 tablespoons butter	1 1/2 pounds green beans
Salt and pepper to taste	1/2 teaspoon chicken bouillon
1/2 teaspoon or less sugar	

Wash beans; cut off tips at both ends. Cut into 1- or 2-inch pieces. Cover with boiling water about 1/2 inch deep; add butter and seasonings. Boil, uncovered, until crispy tender. Most of liquid will be absorbed. Test for doneness and adjust seasonings.

For variety: sauté 1/2 cup chopped onions in the butter; then add to beans along with seasonings to cook. Or add sautéed mushrooms or sliced water chestnuts. Or pour heated sour cream seasoned with onion powder over top to serve.

Pennsylvania Dutch-Style Green Beans

3 strips bacon	2 cups cooked, cut green beans
1 small onion, sliced	2 teaspoons cornstarch
1/4 teaspoon salt	1 hard cooked egg, sliced
1 tablespoon brown sugar	Salt and pepper to taste
1 tablespoon vinegar	1/4 teaspoon dry mustard

Fry bacon strips until crisp; wrap in paper towel to remove grease; crumble. Pour off grease in skillet; add onions: cook until barely soft. Stir in cornstarch, salt, and dry mustard. Drain beans, reserving 1/2 cup liquid. Stir reserved liquid into skillet. Cook, stirring, until mixture boils. Blend in brown sugar and vinegar. Add green beans and heat thoroughly. Turn into serving dish and garnish with egg and crumbled bacon. Makes about 4 servings.

Lima Beans

The name Lima Bean includes several flat-shaped beans that are actually different varieties. There is the Fordhook, a type preferred for freezing, and several other large green varieties usually served fresh. In the dry form, two varieties are most popular—the standard or large dry lima and the baby lima. Actually they are different beans. Only the standard lima has the distinctive nut-like flavor that sets it apart from all others.

The best fresh lima beans are immature and tender, just large enough to be shelled. Also called butter beans, limas are a native of South America.

Choose pods that are bright and unblemished, with no signs of yellowing. Don't buy limp or flabby beans and avoid pods that are too fat. The older beans are tough.

When purchasing in the pod, allow between 1/2 to 3/4 pound per person as a side dish. Place the unwashed pods in a plastic bag in the refrigerator for 2 or 3 days. If you buy the beans already shelled, they should be cooked the same day as purchased.

Limas provide calcium, phosphorus, potassium, magnesium, folic acid, and vitamin A.

Fresh Lima Beans

Shell beans after washing them. Snap off one end of each pod and open pod to remove beans; or cut a thin strip from inner edge of the pod and push beans out.

Cook beans over low heat, covered, in 1 inch boiling water until tender, about 20 minutes. Put a whole onion in the pan when you cook fresh lima beans. It will give a fine flavor to the beans, which then need little else but salt and butter.

Serving ideas: Chill cooked limas and add to chicken, potato, and macaroni salad. Or top hot limas with crumbled sautéed bacon; sour cream seasoned with onion or garlic powder, chopped chives, butler, and diced pimento, sautéed mushrooms with onions. No matter how they are served—on their own or mixed into casseroles, soups, salads—fresh lima beans add a touch of elegance.

Lima Bean Bake

4 slices bacon	4 cups cooked limas
1 large onion, chopped	1 can tomato soup

Sauté bacon; drain; crumble. Brown onion in tablespoon bacon drippings; mix with tomato soup, cooked limas, and bacon. Spoon into 1-quart casserole: sprinkle top with buttered bread crumbs. Bake at 375 degrees until crumbs are brown, about 30 minutes. Serves 6.

Dried Beans

The fact that Boston became famous for its baked beans can be credited to the Puritan prohibition of working on Sunday. Just about everybody in Massachusetts used to bake beans on Saturday for the next day's dinner so they wouldn't have to cook on Sunday. Baked beans, as everybody knows, taste just as good, if not better, the day after they are cooked; so it was an ideal dish to prepare.

Today dried beans are available in a variety of shapes, textures, flavors, and colors. There are black, black-eyed, pink, red, red kidney, pinto, garbanzo, large lima, as well as a variety of white beans such as navy and Great Northern. They are high in protein and complex carbohydrates and dietary fiber, low in fat and sodium.

Many people experience discomfort after eating beans The reason is that beans contain complex sugars that we humans can't digest. What we can't break down, bacteria in our lower intestine can; and in the process, gas is produced. You've heard: "Beans, beans, the musical fruit..." and all that!

Beans are seeds, and the indigestible sugars are nourishment for the seed. One sure way to take the flatulence out of beans is to drop the thoroughly washed beans into boiling water; cook for three minutes; turn off heat, cover and let them soak for a few hours, then pour off and discard water. The heat softens up the seed cell walls that protect the sugars, allowing them to leach more readily into the water. About 65% of the problem is removed—enough to spell relief for most people.

Cooking

Generally speaking, beans should be precooked before being combined with other ingredients. To prepare beans for cooking,

drain off soaking water (this eliminates some of the gas-forming in-gredients); rinse the beans and refill saucepan with fresh water and simmer beans gently until tender. The best way to determine doneness is to taste test; bite into one—it should be tender but firm enough to retain its shape.

As the beans simmer, remove any residue that floats to the top of the water. Add water, as necessary, so beans are always covered.

Flavor with care. Adding herbs and spices early allows the flavor to infuse the beans. But don't add salt or tomatoes to the water until the beans are tender—beans won't soften after these ingredients are added.

Whenever possible, cook the beans a day ahead. Nearly all dried bean dishes are improved by waiting a day or two.

With the fast-food frenzy of modern life, home-cooked dried beans take too long to prepare; time is saved opening a can of beans for preparation of your bean dish.

Dried Bean Basics

If using dried beans, check them carefully before cooking; spread them out on a white towel and discard debris or shriveled beans.

One pound of dried beans equals 2 1/2 cups. When cooked, 1 pound of dried beans measures 5 1/2 to 6 1/2 cups—handy figures to know when substituting canned beans in a dried bean recipe (or vice versa).

Most dried beans need to be rehydrated before cooking. Use either the quick-soaking method or long-soaking method.

Long-soaking method: Use a large pot or bowl, because beans expand when soaked. Cover beans with cold water to level 3 inches above the beans. Soak for several hours or overnight. Drain and use fresh water for cooking the beans.

Quick-soaking method: Place beans in a large pot. Cover with water by at least 3 inches. Bring to boil; immediately reduce heat and simmer for 3 minutes. Remove from heat, cover, and allow to rest for 1 hour. Drain and use fresh water for cooking the beans.

Simmer dried beans: Boiling can cause the liquid to overflow and the beans to break apart.

Salting the beans during cooking slows the cooking and tough-ens the beans. Salt the beans after cooking.

Cooking times for dried beans vary. One way to test for doneness is to squeeze a cooled bean gently between your thumb and index finger. If the core is still hard, cook the beans longer.

A Favorite Baked Bean Recipe

3 strips bacon, cut up	1	pound dried navy beans
1 onion	1	teaspoon prepared mustard
1/2 cup tomato puree	1	teaspoon Worcestershire sauce
Salt to taste	1/4	teaspoon black pepper
2 tablespoons molasses	3	tablespoons brown sugar

Pour 6 cups hot water over washed, cleaned beans; cook for three minutes; turn off heat; cover and let beans soak for a few hours; then pour off and discard water. Add bacon strips and 4 cups fresh water to the beans; bring to boil; simmer 45 minutes.

Mix remaining ingredients, except onion, with some of the bean liquid; stir until smooth; simmer a few minutes; then stir into beans. Place pierced onion in bottom of bean pot; spoon in bean mixture. Cover and bake at 300 degrees about 3 hours until tender. Add more water, if necessary. Makes 6 1/2 cups.

Note: instead of bacon, use strips of salt pork or ham bone.

Stove-Top Version of Baked Beans

2 1/2 ounces salt pork, cubed in small pieces

1 small onion, chopped

1/4 teaspoon ground mustard

Black pepper to taste

1 teaspoon Worcestershire sauce

1/4 cup tomato puree

1 tablespoon molasses

1 1/2 tablespoons brown sugar

2 2/3 tablespoons water

2 cans (about 4 cups) small white beans, drained

In a heavy skillet, lightly brown the salt pork. Add the chopped onion; sauté until translucent. Add mustard, pepper, Worcestershire sauce, and tomato puree. Stir well; simmer about three minutes. Add molasses, brown sugar, and water. Simmer for five minutes. Add beans, stirring gently to mix well without breaking them. Simmer on low heat about 30 minutes. Makes about 8 half-cup servings.

This recipe has only a mild spiciness; if more zing is desired, try adding additional garlic, chili powder, or cloves.

For a vegetarian version, try substituting one-half pound of sliced mushrooms for the pork and sauté the onion and mushrooms in 1 tablespoon vegetable oil.

Beets

Even though beets are related to spinach and chard, they are really root vegetables. For best flavor and tenderness, look for relatively small beets—those from one to two inches in diameter—preferably with tops attached so you can be sure they are fresh. Try to select beets that have young, tender greens in order to have two meals. Use the beet greens the first day; the beets the second day.

Beets provide phosphorus, potassium, magnesium, and vitamin A; beet greens contain calcium, phosphorus, potassium, magnesium, folic acid, and vitamin A.

To prepare, cut off all but 1 inch of beet tops. Wash beets; leave whole with root ends attached; then store in refrigerator. Use within a week. Wash the greens thoroughly in several waters; then use tops as soon as possible, fresh in salads or cooked like spinach. Cook covered, without adding any more water than is on leaves from washing. Cook only a few minutes. Do not overcook. Drain completely; season with salt, pepper, and butter. Beet greens may be chopped and served with sour cream, sprinkled with crumbled bacon pieces; or topped with grated egg; or seasoned with a little vinegar.

To keep beets from fading, cook them unpeeled, with the root ends intact.

To Boil: Heat about 6 cups water to boiling; add beets. Cover and heat to boiling; reduce heat. Cook 40 to 50 minutes or until tender; drain. Run cold water over beets; slip off skins and remove root ends. Slice, dice or cut into thin (Julienne) strips.

To Steam: Place steamer basket in about an inch of water (water should not touch the basket). Place beets in basket. Cover tightly and heat to boiling; reduce heat. Steam about 30 to 50 minutes or until tender. Add boiling water during steaming if necessary. Lift out basket and run cold water over beets; slip off skins and remove ends. Slice, dice, or cut into julienne strips. Steaming produces beets that are moist enough to use in any recipe. It also minimizes bleeding and concentrates flavor.

Depending on size, it is best to quarter very large beets in order to cook them within this time period.

To Roast: Prepare beets same way you would for boiling or steaming. Heat oven to 350 degrees. Wrap beets in foil or brush with olive oil and place in small roasting pan. Roast until tender, about an hour for small to medium beets. Cool slightly and remove skins and stem; serve.

To Microwave: Prepare beets as for other methods. Use microwavable casserole (1 1/2 to 2 quart). Add 1/2 cup water and beets. Cover with lid, or cover with plastic wrap, folding back a 2-inch vent. Microwave 16 to 20 minutes, stirring every 5 minutes until tender.

Beets will continue to cook a short time after microwaving. Let the beets stand 1 or 2 minutes.

Both freshly cooked and canned beets may be served in a variety of interesting ways.

Sautéed Beet Slices

2 tablespoons butter	1 pound can of sliced beets
1 tablespoon sugar	or 2 cups sliced cooked beets

In skillet, melt butter; stir in sugar. Add well-drained beets. Simmer, stirring occasionally, until beets are heated through and slightly glazed. To serve, top with chopped hard-cooked egg. Makes 4 servings.

Beet Salad

1 8-ounce can julienne beets	1/4 teaspoon onion powder
2 tablespoons lemon Jell-O®	2 tablespoons chopped celery
3/4 teaspoon rice vinegar	

Strain beet juice into small saucepan. Bring to boil and stir in Jell-O®. Then add the beets to the Jell-O® mixture. Cool. Stir in chopped celery. Adjust seasonings. Refrigerate until almost set; then spoon into 4 molds. To serve, shred lettuce and spread on individual salad plates; sprinkle with a little gourmet rice vinegar. Unmold beet salad on top of lettuce. Top with teaspoonful of mayonnaise and garnish with a sprig of parsley. Serves 4.

Tiny Red Beets and Pickled Eggs

1 pint young beets	1/2 cup cold water
1/4 cup brown sugar	1/2 teaspoon salt
1/2 cup vinegar	small piece of cinnamon stick
3 or 4 whole cloves	

Cook beets until tender. Drain and skin, reserve juice. While beets are cooking, combine sugar, vinegar, water, salt, cinnamon stick, and cloves. Boil for a few minutes. Pour over skinned beets adding juice to cover. Let beets stand for a few days. Pour juice over shelled, hard-cooked eggs: let eggs stand a couple days in liquid, refrigerated and refrigerate the beets.

These pickled eggs and tiny whole beets are attractive served on a relish plate. Or slice each and spread on top of shredded lettuce topped with a spoonful of salad dressing and sprig of parsley or watercress in center.

Broccoli

Broccoli belongs to the cabbage family, which is listed as a Cruciferous vegetable (a vegetable that has flowers with four petals when in bloom—the four petals look like a crucifix, or cross). The complete list of Cruciferous vegetables includes: broccoli, Brussels sprouts, cabbage, cauliflower, watercress, horseradish, kale, kohlrabi, mustard greens, radish, rutabega, and turnip greens.

The familiar green, closed-headed variety of broccoli has gained popularity for being a member of vegetables reputed to help prevent some cancers. It is important to select heads that have a good color and tightly closed flowerets with no signs of yellowing or browning, and with firm yet tender stocks.

When purchasing broccoli, allow about one quarter pound for each person to be served. Place unwashed broccoli in a plastic bag in refrigerator and use within 3 to 5 days Wash just before using.

Although ounce per ounce, the nutritional value of broccoli flowerets contain nearly eight times as much of the vitamin A-like compound beta-carotene as the stalks, one raw stock provides half the USRDA for vitamin A (according to published letter from Tufts University Diet and Nutrition center). The suggestion is that it would be a shame to throw away the stalk because, like flowerets, it contains B vitamins, vitamin C, calcium, iron and fiber. The Mann Packing Company, in Salinas, California, the world's leading broccoli producer, calls the stems "Heart of Broccoli." The stalk is a rich source of 33 vitamins. But boil it and it will leave much of its nutrients in the pot. So don't throw out the water. Save and use as a healthful base for chowder or soup.

Preparation and Cooking

Trim off any large leaves and cut off the hard end of stock. If stocks are large, cut off flowerets, allowing about 3 inches. Peel the stocks right down to tender flesh; cut off butt ends. Microwaving and steaming are probably the most desirable ways of cooking to getting the full benefits, but there are other cooking methods as well. But avoid sabotaging broccoli's benefits with a heavy sauce such as egg yolk and butter-based hollandaise.

You can cut broccoli stems into various shapes and sizes. Dice and use in tuna or chicken salads, soups, and rice dishes. Shred and substitute for zucchini in zucchini bread or for carrots in carrot muffins. Thinly slice and add to stir-fries, stews, and skillet dishes. Julienne, then stir-fry, steam, or microwave until crisp-tender for a side dish, or omelet filling. Or cut into sticks for dips and snacking.

Flowerets are nice to use as hors d'oeuvres with dips or in tossed green, macaroni, or chef's salad—as well as in various side dishes and casseroles.

A Version of Gerry Conkey's Delicious Broccoli Salad

1/4	cup chopped onion	3	slices chopped bacon, sautéed
1/3	cup golden raisins	1	cup sliced broccoli flowerets
2	tablespoons apple juice	2	cups shredded crisp lettuce

Soak sliced flowerets in ice water; drain. Puff raisins in apple juice in microwave a few seconds; chill and chop. Toss 1 cup of lettuce with all chilled ingredients. Cover and chill. Divide remaining shredded lettuce between 4 chilled salad plates. Carefully stir salad dressing into chilled salad; spoon salad on top of shredded lettuce.

Dressing

1/2	cup mayonnaise	1	tablespoon rice vinegar
1/4	cup chopped pecans	1	tablespoon brown sugar

Stir together mayonnaise, brown sugar, and vinegar. Chill. Stir in chopped pecans; carefully mix into salad ingredients.

Broccoli Flowerets and Carrots

1 bunch broccoli	1 teaspoon onion powder
1 carrot	Salt and pepper to taste
Butter	Sprinkle of NutriSweet®

Scrape and thinly slice carrot: place in bottom of nonstick skillet. Cut broccoli flowerets from stock, reserving stock for another day. Lay bite-size broccoli flowerets on top of carrot slices. Add about 1/2-inch boiling water, a little butter, and seasonings to taste. Bring to boil; cover and quick-cook until vegetables are tender crisp. Liquid will be almost completely absorbed. Shake skillet occasionally to prevent sticking. Pour a little melted butter over top and serve immediately.

Steamed Broccoli

Separate florets from stalks. Cut off woody bottoms from stalks; trim outer peel. Cut length of stock in half; then cut crosswise into bite-size pieces. Arrange the florets and pieces in steamer insert or basket.

Bring about 1 inch water to boil in deep, wide pot. Lower insert or basket with broccoli into pot so it rests above water. Cover and simmer until just tender, 4 1/2 to 5 minutes. Remove broccoli; season as desired or use to proceed with your favorite recipe.

Broccoli Luncheon Special

1 10 ounce package frozen chopped broccoli

1 4 ounce package dried beef, shredded

2 tablespoons butter

2 tablespoons flour

1 cup milk

2 hard-cooked eggs, diced

Toast Cups

Cook broccoli according to package direction; drain.

Cook dried beef with butter until frizzled; blend in flour. Gradually stir in milk to make sauce. Then add broccoli and eggs. Spoon into Toast Cups. Makes 2 2/3 cups.

Toast Cups: Cut crusts from bread slices, brush with melted butter and press slices into 3-inch muffin-pan cups. Toast in moderate oven (350 degrees).

Broccoli Soufflé

4 tablespoons butter	1 cup shredded sharp cheese
4 tablespoons flour	3 eggs, separated
1 cup milk	1 cup cooked, chopped broccoli,
1/4 teaspoon mustard	well drained
Dash cayenne pepper	1/4 teaspoon cream of tartar
Salt and pepper to taste	

Melt the butter. Add the flour, stirring constantly until smooth but not browned. Gradually add the milk to make a thick white sauce. Season with mustard, cayenne, salt, and pepper. Remove from heat and stir in the shredded cheese. Beat the egg yolks well. Drain the broccoli and add along with egg yolks to the cheese mixture. Beat egg whites and cream of tartar until stiff. Fold into cheese mixture. Pour into ungreased 1 1/2 quart oven-proof casserole. Bake at 350 degrees for approximately 50 to 60 minutes or until puffed and golden brown. Serve immediately.

Broccoflower

Since the introduction of broccoflower in October 1988, the green produce is gaining recognition. It is a vitamin-packed genetic cross between broccoli and cauliflower; it has the physical characteristics of cauliflower and the chlorophyll of broccoli. It is beautiful, good-tasting, and nutritious—all qualities that make it fine for the daily diet. It can substitute for broccoli or cauliflower in any favorite recipe normally used for either one. It is very good even in everyday vegetable preparations such as steaming or broiling. In fact for cauliflower, broccoli, and broccoflower, steaming is really the best method of cooking.

Whatever method you choose, avoid over cooking. Not only will flavor remain sweet, but the head will remain whole and attractive. Broccoflower tastes sweeter than cauliflower and has a more textured taste to it.

It is a nice addition to the power-packed cruciferous lineup, such as kohlrabi or mustard greens. Broccoflower shares the fine credentials of the mustard family—including broccoli, cauliflower, Brussels sprouts, kale, and turnips.

To Steam

Place trimmed broccoflower on a steaming rack in a covered pan large enough to accommodate whole head, and cook approximately 15 minutes, watching and testing carefully until a knife can be inserted with only slight resistance. With two wooden spatulas, or even hands protected with oven mitts, carefully remove the head to serving platter. Season with melted butter, salt and pepper, or as desired.

Cauliflower

Just like broccoli, the flowers and stalk are edible. Select a firm, compact head with white or creamy-white, clean flowerets and bright green leaves. Avoid spotted or bruised white edible portion unless it can be trimmed without causing waste. Size of head does not affect quality. If leaves have grown through the head, they affect the appearance only.

Cauliflower is a good source of vitamin C and a fair source of iron.

Many people like to serve the flowerets raw for dippers or in salads, but cauliflower can be steamed, baked, or sautéed. It can be cooked whole or broken into flowerets. It also pickles well.

Basic Preparation: Cut away the woody base and tough outer leaves. Tender green leaves may be left on or saved and used as salad greens. The head may be left whole or separated into flowerets. Wash in cold running water, holding head or flowerets upside down.

Have about 1 Inch of water boiling in a saucepan. Add 1/2 teaspoon salt per cup or head. A slice of lemon or a little lemon juice added to the water helps keep cauliflower white. Cook for 5 minutes, uncovered, then cover. Flowerets cook in 5 to 10 minutes; heads in 15 to 20 minutes. Do not overcook or cauliflower will discolor.

Boiled Cauliflower

Select a white, tightly packed head without spots or bruises. Remove leaves and woody stem. Separate into flowerets or leave whole; wash thoroughly. To retain whiteness, soak a few minutes in cold water with a little lemon juice added. Drain and place in a small amount of slightly salted boiling water. Cover and cook until just tender but still crisp. Do not overcook. Drain; season to taste; serve with butter, a cheese sauce, or sauce of choice. One medium-sized head (about 2 pounds) makes 5 to 6 servings.

Steamed Cauliflower Flowerets

Trim off leaves and cut out core. Cut cauliflower into flowerets; wash thoroughly. Soak in cold water with lemon juice. Drain and place in steamer over boiling water, making sure the water does not touch the basket. When steaming process begins, cover and steam about 15 minutes until flowerets are tender-crisp. Sprinkle with salt. Just before serving in heated dish, pour over a little melted butter. Add a sprinkle of freshly chopped parsley. Or top with grated cheddar cheese.

Brussels Sprouts

Choose the smallest size young Brussels sprouts available with firm, compact heads of uniform size. Allow about 3 sprouts for each person to be served (or for serving 4 people allow 1 1/2 pounds fresh sprouts or a 10-ounce package frozen sprouts).

When you get home, pull off and dispose of any loose, broken or yellow leaves. Put the sprout heads, unwashed, into a plastic bag and refrigerate. Use within 2 or 3 days.

To prepare and cook to perfection: Remove any undesirable leaves from sprouts; wash thoroughly. Cut stems off close to heads, but not so close that leaves will fall off. With paring knife, cut "X" in stem ends to ensure more even cooking. In saucepan over high heat, in 1-inch boiling water, heat Brussels sprouts to boiling. Reduce heat to low; cover and simmer about 10 minutes or until tender-crisp. Season as desired.

Brussels Sprouts and Carrot Cubes

2 carrots	1 1/2 pounds fresh Brussels sprouts
Pinch of sugar	Salt and pepper to taste
2 cups chicken broth	1 tablespoon or more of butter

Scrape and slice carrots into about 1/2-inch slices. Set aside. In saucepan cook sprouts in chicken broth until barely fork tender. Drain sprouts, reserving the broth; keep warm.

Add seasonings to the broth; add carrot slices and cook until just tender. Drain broth into skillet: adjust seasonings; boil down to 1/3 clip; stir in butter until melted: add the carrots and sprouts; toss lightly; heat thoroughly and serve immediately. Serves 4.

Cabbage

Next to potatoes, cabbage is the world's second most popular vegetable. Whether you select green, red, Chinese, or a non-heading variety such as bok choy, you are choosing a vegetable that is an excellent source of vitamin C, a good source of vitamin A, a fine source of fiber, and a fair source of minerals. Raw cabbage is, of course, more nutritious than cooked. To best retain its nutritive value, cabbage should not be overcooked.

There are endless possibilities for this versatile vegetable. Cut into wedges and steam. Or after shredding it, either coarsely or finely, leave it raw for salads or slaws, or cook in soups. The leaves can be steamed and stuffed. The head can be hollowed out and stuffed and cooked, or it can be left raw and used for serving dips.

Red cabbage, also widely available, is a little sweeter than the green variety. It is popular for its vibrant color. To retain that rich color, add vinegar or lemon juice to raw red cabbage for salads. Add vinegar, lemon juice, or another acidic ingredient (apple slices work too) to the water when cooking red cabbage.

Cooking Method for Cabbage

Important rule in cooking cabbage is "do it quickly." Use no more water than about one-third the amount of cabbage. Quartered cabbage takes only 7 to 12 minutes; shredded cabbage, 3 to 7 minutes. Add the salt after the cabbage comes to a boil.

Cabbage does not develop a strong flavor if it is not overcooked. It is mild and sweet in flavor when shredded and cooked quickly and briefly with a little butter and a few tablespoons of water in a covered skillet. Watch the heat and cook only until vegetable is tender-crisp. Cooked by this method, cabbage will retain 90% of the vitamin C.

Sweet-Sour Cabbage

2 tablespoons butler	5 cups shredded cabbage
1/4 cup water	3/4 teaspoon chicken bouillon
2 tablespoons vinegar	2 tablespoons brown sugar
1 tablespoon cornstarch	1/2 cup sautéed diced bacon

Cook cabbage quickly in a very little boiling water, adding a little salt, until crispy tender. Melt butter; stir in sugar, 2 tablespoons water, vinegar, add chicken bouillon. Make a paste of remaining 2 tablespoons water and cornstarch; add hot mixture, stirring until thick and clear. Add sautéed bacon pieces. Pour over cabbage and serve. Serves 6.

Cole Slaw

This strange name comes to us from the Dutch word "koolsla." In Dutch, "kool" means cabbage and "sla" means salad—and that is what cole slaw is!

2 tablespoons vinegar	6 cups shredded cabbage
2 tablespoons sugar	1/2 cup dairy sour cream
1/2 teaspoon salt	Green pepper rings

Soak shredded cabbage in ice water until crisp. Drain thoroughly. Mix remaining ingredients together; pour over cabbage; mix well. Garnish with green pepper rings. Serves 8.

Cole Slaw

4 cups shredded cabbage	1/2 cup shredded carrots
1/4 cup chopped celery	Green and red pepper rings

Combine cabbage, carrots, and celery. Cover and refrigerate until well chilled. Blend in chilled Sweet–Sour Cream Dressing. Spoon cole slaw into chilled bowl lined with lettuce leaves. Garnish with green and red pepper slices.

Sweet-Sour Cream Dressing

1/4 cup brown sugar	1/4 cup gourmet rice vinegar
1/4 cup dairy sour cream	1/2 teaspoon onion powder
1/4 teaspoon dill	1/8 teaspoon black pepper
Salt to taste	

Combine brown sugar, vinegar, and spices; bring to boil, stirring until sugar dissolves. Boil about 1 minute. Chill. Stir in sour cream and salt to taste. Cover and chill. Serves 6.

Confetti Slaw

1 small grated carrot	1/2 small head cabbage, shredded
1 tablespoon grated onion	1/4 head red cabbage, shredded
1/4 cup snipped parsley	1/3 cup chopped green pepper
1/4 cup raisins, optional	1 small apple, grated

Combine chilled ingredients; toss with chilled Dressing. Spoon onto chilled shredded lettuce on salad plates. Serves 6 to 8.

Dressing

2 teaspoons sugar	1/3 cup Miracle Whip®
Salt and pepper to taste	2 teaspoons rice vinegar

Combine ingredients. Cover. Chill.

Turkey Stuffed Cabbage Leaves

Rice:

- 1 large onion, finely chopped
- 2 teaspoons olive oil
- 2/3 cup water
- 3 tablespoons uncooked long-grain white rice
- 1/4 teaspoon salt and a pinch of pepper

Cabbage:

- 6 large cabbage leaves from green cabbage

Cabbage Stuffing:

- 12 ounces ground turkey
- 1/2 teaspoon dill weed
- 1 egg
- 1/4 teaspoon leaf marjoram, crumbled
- 1/4 teaspoon salt
- 1/8 teaspoon pepper
- 1/2 small carrot, peeled, halved lengthwise and very thinly sliced
- 1 cup chicken broth
- 2 tablespoons butter, cut up

Prepare rice: Sauté onion in small saucepan over medium-low heat, 5 minutes. Add 3 tablespoons water; cook until water has evaporated and onion is soft, about 4 minutes. Remove and reserve 1/3 cup onion.

Add rice to saucepan; stir to coat. Add remaining water, salt and pepper. Cover and cook until rice is tender and liquid is absorbed, about 7 minutes.

Preheat oven to hot (400 degrees).

Blanch cabbage leaves in large pot of boiling salted water for 1 minute. Drain; transfer to paper toweling to dry.

Prepare Cabbage Stuffing: Combine turkey, dill, egg, marjoram, salt, pepper; and rice mixture in medium-sized bowl. Place 1 cabbage leaf in small ladle or custard cup, rib-side down and ends of leaf hanging over sides. Spoon about 1/3 cup of turkey mixture into leaf-lined ladle; fold ends over filling, packing it down. Turn out into palm of hand; place round cabbage packet in 11 by 7-inch baking pan. Repeat with remaining leaves and filling. Sprinkle carrot and reserved onion into pan. Pour in broth. Cover pan with aluminum foil.

Bake in hot oven (400) degrees) for 30 minutes or until bubbly and filling is firm.

Remove cabbage packets with slotted spoon to platter. Pour broth mixture into saucepan. Cook over high heat until slightly reduced. Lower heat to medium; swirl in butter until sauce appears creamy. Pour over cabbage. Serves 6.

Carrots

Carrots are probably the most versatile of all the vegetables. They are naturals for easy fixings; they need only a good scraping or thin paring before cooking or eating raw. They can be cooked whole, sliced, diced, shredded, or as sticks; they can be served alone or combined with other vegetables; they can be baked, creamed, or buttered; they can be served as a main dish, salad, appetizer, a garnish, or a between-meal nibble.

Carrots are rich in beta carotene, which the body converts to vitamin A. You can get the most beta-carotene out of foods if you cook them rather than eating them raw—absorption is higher when the fibrous tissue is softened. And beta-carotene is not harmed by freezing or microwaving. Carrots also contain some B vitamins. They are a very good source of potassium and they offer a lot of fiber.

When you purchase carrots, allow about 1/3 pound for each side dish you are preparing.

Remove carrot tops before storing. Place unwashed carrots in a plastic bag in refrigerator; they'll keep for several weeks.

But be sure to store them away from apples, bananas, and pears.

These fruits naturally give off a gas called ethylene oxide and will make carrots stored near them taste bitter. If you are purchasing baby-cut carrots or sticks rather than whole carrots, they must be stored away from those fruits also. They have a shorter shelf life (up to 14 days; if they develop that weird white coating, just rinse them in ice water to get rid of it).

If you're not a fan of carrot sticks, you'll be pleased to know that carrots cooked in a bit of fat are actually better for you than raw. That is because beta-carotene is fat-soluble, so that touch of butter or oil makes it easier for the body to absorb. Carrots cooked until tender-crisp deliver more beta-carotene than raw ones.

The carrot does need some embellishment because it tends to be bland. But with a little extra seasoning, it is a very desirable vegetable and its bright color adds eye appeal to any menu.

Cook carrots in a minimum of liquid so the liquid simmers down to a self-making sauce or glaze. Like all vegetables it is important not to overcook them.

Glazed Carrots

1 pound carrots	2 tablespoons butter
Salt to taste	1 tablespoon brown sugar

Scrape carrots; cut diagonally into 1/4-inch slices. Combine ingredients; add small amount of water; cook until carrots are crispy-tender. On high, cook, stirring constantly, until liquid is evaporated and carrots are glazed. Serve hot. Serves 3.

Buttered Carrots

Scrub carrots thoroughly and scrape lightly to remove only the outer layer of skin. Tiny young carrots may be left whole for cooking; but older carrots should be sliced lengthwise in halves or quarters, or sliced crosswise. Barely cover with boiling salted water (1/4 teaspoon salt to each 1 cup water). Cover and gently cook until just tender, about

10 minutes, depending on size and age of carrots and how they are cut. Remove cover; add a little butter; evaporate remaining liquid, watching carefully to avoid scorching. Season with onion powder, pinch of sugar, pepper; or adjust seasonings to suit taste.

For creamed carrots, add a little rich cream or medium white sauce to cooked carrots; heat through and serve. For carrots and peas, add crisp cooked buttered peas to the cooked carrots; serve hot.

Carrot Patties

1 tablespoon flour	1 egg plus 1 egg white
3/4 pound carrots	1 tablespoon brown sugar
1 tablespoon butter	Pinch of salt

Scrape and finely shred the carrots. Combine whole egg, flour, brown sugar, and butter; beat until well blended; stir in carrots.

Whip egg white with salt until stiff; quickly fold into carrot mixture, being careful to not deflate the white too much.

Brush a heated non-stick skillet with butter; drop 1/4-cup mounds of batter onto hot griddle; flatten a bit with back of spatula. Fry on both sides until golden brown. Serves 4.

To serve with the meat course, add 1 tablespoon minced parsley, diced shallot, and 1/2 teaspoon minced fresh tarragon to the mixture before folding in whipped egg white.

Baked Grated Carrots

3 cups shredded or grated carrots	1/2 teaspoon salt (or to suit taste)
3 tablespoons butter	1/2 teaspoon sugar
1/8 teaspoon pepper	

Place carrots in buttered casserole; season with sugar, salt, and pepper; dot with butter; cover. Do not add water. Bake at 375 degrees about 30 minutes, or until barely tender. Serves 5 to 6.

These carrots are especially attractive shaped into a nest and center filled with hot buttered green peas. If plate service, make individual nests on each plate

Carrot-Raisin Salad

3 cups grated carrots	6 tablespoons dairy sour cream
1 cup seedless raisins	1 tablespoon rice vinegar
1 tablespoon brown sugar	Dash of salt

Puff raisins in vinegar a few seconds in microwave oven. Chill. Mix chilled raisins and carrots. Blend together sugar, salt, and sour cream; pour over carrots and raisins; toss lightly to mix. Serve as is, or spoon into lettuce cups, salad style.

Carrot Slaw

1 cup shredded carrots	1 cup shredded crisp cabbage
1/4 cup raisins	1 tablespoon orange liqueur
1/4 teaspoon salt	2 tablespoons rice vinegar
1 tablespoon sugar	1/4 cup Miracle Whip®

Sprinkle liqueur over raisins in custard cup; cover and puff in microwave oven a few seconds, stirring once. Chill. Combine carrots, cabbage and raisins. Blend remaining ingredients; pour over vegetables; toss to mix. Spoon onto lettuce leaf on chilled salad plate. Garnish with sprig of parsley.

Corn

An ear of corn always has an even number or rows of kernels. Odd, isn't it?

The fresher the corn the better. Keep corn refrigerated and unhusked until just before cooking.

Do not add salt when cooking corn on the cob. Salt toughens the corn; so does overcooking. For extra sweetness, add a little sugar to cooking water.

Kettle-Cooked Corn on the Cob

Remove husks and silk. Snap or cut off ends of any imperfect ear. Rinse in cold water. Then proceed to cook in either of following two ways:

1—Plunge the ears into vigorously boiling unsalted water; add 1/2 cup milk and; about 1 teaspoon sugar. Make sure water completely covers the corn; bring to boiling. Immediately cover the kettle and turn off the heat. Let corn stand in water 6 to 7 minutes, depending on maturity of the corn. Drain and serve immediately with softened butter, salt and pepper.

2—Place the corn in kettle with a pinch of sugar and just enough cold water to cover. Don't put salt into the water. When water just comes to a boil, toss in teaspoon of salt; drain immediately and the corn will be cooked tender and ready to eat. You don't need to time it or test it. If you start with cold water, it will be cooked when water boils—and corn will be juicy.

Microwave Corn on the Cob

The ears can be cooked in the husk; if they have been husked, wrap in waxed paper or microwaveable plastic wrap. For one medium ear, microwave on high 3 to 5 minutes, turning over once. Let stand, wrapped, 1 minute. For 2 ears, microwave on high 4 to 9 minutes, turning once. Let stand, wrapped, 1 to 2 minutes.

To test for doneness, press kernels with fingers or a utensil; the kernels should be slightly resistant. They will became more tender during the standing time.

Corn, Ham, and Cheese Soufflé (Very special)

Coat a 1 1/2-quart oven-proof dish (or four 20-ounce dishes) with butter. Sprinkle with fine Ritz® cracker crumbs. Set aside.

1 1/2 cups frozen petite white corn kernels

1/3 cup thinly sliced, chopped red onion

3 ounces (about 2/3 cup) maple-glazed ham, grated

1/4 cup all-purpose flour

3/4 cup 1% milk

2 ounces New York State sharp Cheddar cheese, grated

1/4 teaspoon ground black pepper

Pinch of salt

2 egg yolks

4 egg whites

1/2 teaspoon cream of tartar

Coat a large nonstick skillet with butter; place over medium-high

heat until hot. Add chopped onions; sauté until barely tender; stir in corn, stirring until heated through; remove from heat; stir in grated ham. Set aside.

Place the flour in a small saucepan. Gradually add milk, stirring until blended, cook over medium heat about 3 minutes, stirring constantly, until thickened. Remove from heat; stir in cheese and pepper.

Beat egg yolks in a medium bowl at high speed of a mixer until thick and pale (about 5 minutes). Gradually add hot milk mixture to egg yolks, stirring constantly. Stir in corn mixture; set aside.

Be sure egg whites are at room temperature. Beat egg whites, pinch of salt, and cream of tartar in a large bowl at high speed or a mixer. Gently fold beaten egg whites into egg yolk-corn mixture.

Pour mixture into prepared soufflé dish (or into the four oven-proof dishes). Bake on lower shelf or a 325-degree preheated oven for about 1 hour until puffed and golden. Less time for individuals. Serves 4.

(Yes, it takes time to prepare; but it's worth the effort.)

Eggplant

Most of us think of eggplant as the deep purple variety with a creamy textured flesh. But it actually got its name from the white-skinned variety that tastes like the familiar purple one. The only difference is that white eggplants turn gray when they are cooked.

There are more than 50 varieties of eggplant, and they come in myriad shapes, sizes, and colors. It is important that the eggplant has not reached its maximum size for best flavor.

Eggplant growers will find this information from *Science News* of interest: "Keep a close eye on your eggplants and note the date when the fruits start to form. The best time to pick the crop will be exactly six weeks later. Food scientists in Spain have found that sugar levels in eggplants increase through the end of the sixth week and then drop dramatically over the next 10 days. Other important flavor compounds follow the same cycle, dropping precipitously after the 42nd day."

The large eggplants usually sold in supermarkets have more flesh than the Japanese eggplant. Check when buying! The fewer seeds in an eggplant the less bitter it tastes and that depends on the eggplant's sex. Check the end opposite the stem; there you will find a beige colored "scar" or indentation. If this "scar" is oblong, the eggplant is female and will have lots of seeds. A small round "scar" is a male and will have far fewer seeds.

No matter what cooking method is used, eggplant always comes out firmer, browner, and sweeter when cooked slowly rather than quickly.

All types of eggplant can be interchanged—Japanese, Italian, or white. It is just a question of which size and shape is appropriate for your recipe. No matter which type you use, the skin should be tight and the flesh firm.

Pan–Fried Eggplant

I small eggplant	Seasonings to taste:
I beaten egg	sugar, onion powder, pepper
1 tablespoon water	1 cup cracker crumbs

Beat egg, water, and seasoning together. Pare eggplant; slice 1/2-inch thick: cut into 1/2-wide strips. (Or use the slender Japanese eggplant and just slice crosswise.) Dip slices into egg mixture: and then dip into cracker crumbs. In non-stick skillet, shallow-fry in butter or bacon grease until golden brown on both sides. Nice served with pan-fried tomato slices.

Oven–Crisped Eggplant

1/2 cup finely rolled cracker crumbs	1 egg
	1 tablespoon water
1/4 teaspoon oregano	2 1-pound eggplants
1/2 teaspoon paprika	1/2 teaspoon salt
1/4 cup melted butter	

Crush crackers into very fine crumbs between two pieces of waxed paper with rolling pin; mix with oregano, paprika and salt. Set aside. Beat egg with water. Peel eggplants and cut lengthwise into six segments each. Dip eggplant pieces into beaten egg and then crumb mixture. Let stand 30 minutes to set crumb coating.

Place peeled side down, in shallow baking pan. Spoon melted butter over pieces. Bake in 400-degree oven for 20 minutes or until crisp on the outside and tender on the inside. Makes 6 servings.

Eggplant Meatloaf

1 medium eggplant	1 pound lean ground beef
2 eggs	1 medium onion, minced
1 cup cracker crumbs	1/2 cup finely chopped parsley
1/2 teaspoon thyme	Salt and pepper to taste
1/4 cup ketchup	Sprinkle of onion powder

Peel and cube eggplant; simmer in a very little salted water until soft; mash and cool. Stir in all remaining ingredients except ketchup and onion powder; mix thoroughly. Spoon mixture into buttered meatloaf pan. Spread ketchup over top and sprinkle lightly with onion powder. Bake in 350 degree oven about 1 hour. Serve garnished with tomato slices. Serves 6.

Ratatouille Baked in Individual Foil Packets

1 tablespoon butter	2 cups sliced zucchini
1/2 cup sliced onion	1/2 cup sliced green pepper
1 teaspoon sugar	1/4 cup chopped parsley
1/4 cup tomato paste	Salt and pepper to taste
2 cups diced eggplant	1/2 teaspoon dried thyme
2 slices crumbled, sautéed bacon	

Place onions and butter in oven-proof container; cover and microwave a few seconds until tender, stirring once. Stir in tomato paste and seasonings. Carefully stir into combined vegetables and crumbled bacon pieces. Spoon onto center of 4 pieces of heavy aluminum foil; form into packets, sealing tightly. Place on baking sheet. Bake in 425- to 450-degree oven 20 to 25 minutes until vegetables are crispy tender. Serve in packets. (If you prefer vegetables more tender, let set a few minutes before serving.)

Note: These packets may also be placed on a grill over moderately hot coals. Grill about 20 minutes for crisp-tender vegetables.

Garlic

Folklore projects garlic as magical, mystical, and medicinal. To those who adore the taste of garlic, it is the king of seasonings. But those who have a deep dislike for this pungent plant often quote an old proverb which says, "Garlic makes men wink, drink, and stink."

Although there are claims that garlic aids digestion, it is more often blamed for triggering heartburn and indigestion in the susceptible. If the use of garlic causes gastrointestinal discomfort, it clearly does not agree with a person. But those who can tolerate garlic thoroughly enjoy the flavor to perk up soups, salads, casseroles, meat entrees, sauces, and much more.

Garlic, a member of the lily family properly called *Allium sativum*, grows in little clusters called bulbs, or heads. As a rule, each bulb contains 1 to 20 individual cloves, enclosed in a white skin.

Fresh Garlic Hints

When purchasing: Look for clean, dry, firm garlic heads with unbroken papery outer skits and no shoots.

Storing: Keep garlic in a cool, dry place with good circulation, not in refrigerator. The perforated clay crocks made especially for storing garlic provide the combination of darkness and air circulation that help keep it fresh.

Heat and handling affect garlic's potency. Raw garlic is stronger in flavor than cooked garlic. The longer garlic cooks, the more delicate the flavor. Whole cloves and large pieces give off a gentler flavor than cut, minced, or mashed garlic.

If you object to the odor of garlic on your breath, remember it usually comes from eating raw garlic. When your breath may make a difference, stick to cooked forms; cooked garlic won't linger as long or as strongly.

Bad breath or smelly fingers are a price you pay for a garlic dining experience. Various suggestions are given for both conditions, which are partially curable but not necessarily foolproof.

Suggestions to get rid of garlic breath: chew parsley or fennel, natural breath fresheners; drink lemon juice; chase with a lot of mint-flavored tooth paste and mouth wash.

To get rid of odor on hands: rinse hands with salt, lemon, or lime juice, and rinse under cold water; rub hands in used coffee grounds; rub hands thoroughly with toothpaste (instead of soap) and wash in warm water; wash your hands with a paste of baking soda and mild water.

Flavors

Garlic offers a variety of flavors, depending on how you handle it. The slender clove can have a meek, onion-like flavor where it is used raw, unpeeled, and whole. The intense flavor and fragrance comes from peeling and mincing garlic.

What accounts for the variations and nuances in its flavor is a chemical reaction that occurs when the tissue cells are disturbed. When garlic clove is in its original state, whole and covered with a double layer of paper skin, it has a subtle flavor and mild aroma. Slicing that same clove causes an enzyme reaction, resulting in the creation of diallyl sulfide, the primary culprit in garlic odor. The more you break down the tissue cells by peeling, chopping, or mashing the clove, the more pronounced the garlic flavor and odor. This holds true for the three most popular varieties of garlic, available according to the season in the marketplace. The white-fleshed Californian, the purple-tinged Mexican, and the dark-tinged Argentinian can be used interchangeably.

Elephant garlic (or Tahitian garlic), a hybrid now available in limited quantities, has extra-large cloves (can be as big as a grapefruit). It looks just like its smaller counterpart, but, besides being larger, it has a milder flavor and not such an overpowering garlicky aroma. Because of its mild flavor, elephant garlic can be used thinly sliced—rather than chopped or minced—to provide more even flavoring in dishes. And it can be used raw in salads and sandwiches. Whole cloves can be roasted like small onions and potatoes along with meat entrees. Or, it can be sautéed with fresh vegetables and also added to pasta, sauces, and stews.

Using garlic raw: Hit the clove sharply with the flat part of a knife so the skin splits, then remove it. And here is the way to cut down on your garlic chopping chores! Mince a whole head of garlic at once. Because that is enough garlic to season 40 dishes (or 400, or 4,000, depending on your taste), it is necessary to find some means of preserving it. Loose-pack freezing is one of the easiest ways. Simply spread the chopped garlic bits in a layer on a waxed paper-covered cookie sheet; freeze so they don't clump together; then put the frozen pieces into a plastic bag or freezer container and store in freezer for future use.

You also can freeze whole heads of garlic with the cloves intact without any preparation. Place the whole head of garlic in a plastic bag and put in freezer. The nice part is the cloves will expand just enough as they freeze to pop off of their skins with no peeling needed. The self-peeled garlic clove can be added whole to a stew, soup, or other long-cooking dish.

Garlic Tips

Garlic in Salad Dressing: Just peel and drop the clove into the dressing. The vinegar will extract the flavor.

Sautéing: Preheat oil or butter over medium-low to medium heat, add garlic, and stir constantly to prevent burning. Or sauté whole, peeled cloves in same way, then remove the cloves, leaving a garlic flavor in the oil.

Fresh Garlic Substitutes

Dried seasonings are handy substitutes. Any of these garlic products—garlic powder, garlic salt, instant minced garlic or garlic chips, liquid garlic, and garlic juice—may be used according to individual tastes.

A 1/8 teaspoon garlic powder, instant minced garlic, or garlic chips are equivalent to 1 average-size clove of fresh garlic.

When using garlic powder in a recipe with a high acid content, a more distinctive garlic flavor may he obtained by moistening the garlic powder in water before adding; use 1/4 teaspoon water to 1/8 teaspoon garlic powder.

A 1/2 teaspoon garlic salt is equivalent to 1 average-size garlic clove, but decrease the amount of salt called for in the recipe.

Garlic chips may be used in recipes where small pieces of garlic are desirable. Liquid should be used sparingly, as this is concentrated in flavor: one drop or more, to suit individual taste. Garlic juice has a milder flavor and can be used for giving just a hint of garlic.

Dry Onions

The onion plant is related to the lily. The onion is one of the most widely consumed and one of the most versatile of all the cultivated vegetables. It can be shredded, chopped, stuffed, sliced, or diced before being sautéed, puréed, baked, boiled, blanched, braised, and

creamed to mention a few. In addition, this versatile vegetable doubles as a flavoring agent and adds depth to salads, soups, stews, stocks, and sauces.

A great variety of onions exists—red, white, and yellow, flat or torpedo-shaped, from marble-sized to enormous. There are yellow onions, white onions, and three fairly sweet ones: red Italian, Bermuda, Spanish. Yellow are all-purpose; whites are primarily used whole as a vegetable course or in stews; red Italians are usually served raw, in salads; Bermudas, too, lend themselves to salads, to baking, and, like the Spanish, to marvelous French-frying. New favorites are the very mild summer onions—Walla Wallas from Washington state, Vidalias from Georgia, the Kulasweet Maui, and the Texan X-33s. Due to their high water content, these sweet varieties do not store well. They also have less of the sulfur compound that gives onions their characteristic pungency. Sweet summer onions are so mild you can bite into them like crunchy apples.

Burgundy is a large onion with beautiful dark-red skin; it has a sweet, mild flavor, but not as mild as Walla Walla Sweets or the other three sweet onions, but they are less expensive, are good keepers, and will store well for several months. Slices of it are nice on hamburgers, and it makes an attractive addition to a salad.

There's a little trick to dealing with onions, even the sweet onions—refrigeration. A sliced onion that has been cooled will taste sweeter than a fresh onion at room temperature, apparently because the cooling affects the acids that produce the onion character—the cooling increases the sweetness.

Store whole onions in open brown grocery bags in the refrigerator; onions last longer and do not sprout as quickly. As long as they are not cut, they give off no odor. And a big plus—you will not cry when you chop a refrigerated onion. Once the onion is cut, wrap in plastic wrap or a covered plastic storage container and refrigerate. Your cut onion will keep for several days. Or chopped onions may be placed in a covered shallow pan and frozen.

Scallions and green onions are used interchangeably in recipes. Technically the difference is that green onions have a definite bulb formation, while scallions are any shoots from the white onion varieties that are pulled before the bulb has formed.

Onions discolor if they are cooked in an aluminum or iron pot, or are sliced with a carbon-steel knife. Red onions, like red cabbage, contain pigments that turn redder in acid (lemon juice, vinegar) and bluish in a basic (alkaline) solution.

A handy tip for peeling pearl onions (shallots and garlic too) is to blanch them in boiling water for about 10 seconds, then cool under cold running water. The outermost skin will slip right off.

Research indicates that it is oil released from bruising an onion that causes eyes to tear and noses to stream. Refrigerate the onions or soak them in ice water before chopping. Then use a very sharp knife and work quickly, since pungent oils will be released as the onion warns up.

To turn strong-tasting yellow onions into mild sweet ones, slice them thinly into a bowl and pour boiling water over; drain and chill. They will be crisp and almost as mild as the big sweet, Spanish onions. Or to make raw onion rings less strong for use in salads, soak slices in cold water for an hour.

Conventional techniques call for cooking onions in fat until they soften. But the onion absorbs the fat as it cools and becomes high in calories as well as hard to digest. It is the heat, not the fat that causes them to soften. The trick is to cook them in a little bit of moisture (water, broth, or wine) and add a bit of oil or butter last minute to aid in browning.

Baked Onion Rings

Easy to make and deliciously crisp, these onion rings are baked instead of deep-fried.

Lightly beat 2 large egg whites with 1/2 teaspoon salt, 1/4 teaspoon sugar, and 1/8 teaspoon pepper. Slice a large, peeled, sweet yellow onion into 1/4-inch thick slices and separate into rings. Place 1/3 cup finely ground Ritz® cracker crumbs on waxed paper. Using tongs or fork, dip onion rings into egg white, one at a time, turning to completely coat; then dip in crumbs, turning to coat well. Place rings on ungreased non-stick baking sheet in a single layer. Bake about 10 minutes in a 450-degree oven.

Sweet Peppers

Sweet peppers, or bell peppers as they are commonly known because of their shape, come in shades or green, red, yellow, and

purple. Green peppers, green at first, change when ripe to red or yellow, depending on variety. The purple variety (mellow in flavor) was developed by the same people who produced tulips in a rainbow of shades, the Dutch. The purple variety turns green when cooked. Red and yellow peppers won't fade in cooking since their carotenoid pigments are impervious to normal heat.

All peppers are highly nutritious, containing appreciable amounts of vitamin C and A, as well as the mineral potassium. They are endearingly non-fattening too; an average medium size contains about 15 calories. Although the red pepper has a higher calorie count than the green, it also boasts twice the vitamin C and more than 10 times the vitamin A. The yellow pepper is similar in shape, flavor, and nutrition to the red pepper, but the red pepper is sweeter. Green peppers are picked earlier and they have a somewhat sharper taste.

When choosing sweet peppers, make sure the skin is uniformly firm and shiny with no soft or wrinkled spots. The interior ribs and seeds should be removed before eating or cooking.

Bell peppers are extremely versatile and can be used as a shell for stuffing or to hold dips and sauces. They can be roasted and peeled, grilled with meats and fish, sautéed with other vegetables, stir-fried or served raw in a salad or as snacks. For visual impact and wonderful flavor, try combining green, red, and yellow peppers together in a salad or chicken dish. Use your imagination and see if you can come up with interesting ways to use peppers—raw or cooked.

The Takano Fruit Parlor in Tokyo came up with a clever product: they sell "Salad Sausages," sausages made of bell peppers, squash, zucchini, carrots, onions—a dozen different veggie wieners in all—no meats in the sausages.

Fascinating Facts

Sometimes two forms of the same food can differ in vitamin A. Sweet red peppers, the ripe form of common green peppers, are about eight times richer in vitamin A.

And it is interesting to note ounce for ounce, raw red peppers have four times more vitamin C than peeled oranges.

Fried Green Pepper Rings

2 large green peppers
1 egg
1 tablespoon water
Peanut oil

3/8 cup fine cracker crumbs
1/2 teaspoon chicken stock base
Salt and pepper to taste

Wash peppers; cut off tops; remove seeds and ribs; cut into 1/4-inch rings; rinse thoroughly in cold water; completely dry on paper towels. Dip rings in crumbs mixed with seasonings, dip in egg beaten with water; and dip again in the crumbs. Chill about 1 hour. Use enough oil to give 1/2-inch depth in pan. Heat oil to 370 or 375 degrees. Fry pepper rings in the hot oil until lightly browned on both sides; drain on paper towels. Serve hot. Nice served with steaks or chops. Makes 4 servings.

Sautéed Peppers

Choose from green and sharp, red and sweet, yellow and fruity, or purple and mellow peppers. Sauté with minced onion in a bit of butter, seasoned with salt, pepper, and spice of choice and serve as an accompaniment to poached fish.

Stir–Fried Chicken with Red Pepper and Pea Pods

1 red pepper
4 scallions
1 tablespoon dry sherry
1/2 cup orange juice
1/4 cup peanut oil

2 large chicken breasts
1/2 cup edible pod peas
2 1/2 teaspoons cornstarch
1 teaspoon minced peeled ginger
1 tablespoon soy sauce

Bone, skin, split, and cut chicken into 1 1/2- by 1/2-inch strips. Mix soy sauce, sherry, sliced scallions, and ginger. Add chicken strips; toss well; set aside. Combine orange juice and cornstarch; set aside.

Snip ends and strip edible pod peas. Cut red pepper in half and remove ribs and seeds; cut pepper into strips.

Heat the 1/4 cup oil in large skillet. Stir-fry chicken with marinade until thick and loses its color, about 2 minutes. Add pea pods and green pepper strips: stir-fry 2 minutes. Stir orange juice mixture; add to chicken; stir-fry until slightly thickened. Serve immediately. Serves 4.

Pepper Stuffing

Any kind of leftover cooked meat or poultry may be used in the vegetable stuffing. Or use a savory blend of lean ground beef, pork, and veal combined with a little instant rice for lightness and season with condensed tomato soup rather than fresh tomatoes, onion powder, salt, pepper, and a pinch of sugar.

Vegetable Stuffed Peppers

6	green peppers	1 1/2	cups petite white corn
1	cup diced tomatoes	2	slightly beaten eggs
2	tablespoons melted butter	1/2	teaspoon sugar
1/4	cup finely minced onion		Salt and pepper to taste
1/2	cup soft bread crumbs	1/4	cup finely minced celery

Cut green peppers in half lengthwise: remove seeds and ribs. Precook peppers a couple minutes in boiling water; invert and drain on towel. Combine other ingredients; stuff peppers with mixture. Place in large greased casserole; add small amount of water; cover and bake at 350 degrees about 1 hour.

Potatoes

The "fattening" reputation the potato has suffered for years is unfair because an average-size potato, served plain, has only about 100 calories—about the same as a large apple, or 1/2 cup cottage cheese, rice, noodles, or bran flakes. Potatoes do contain starch, and too much can be fattening. But potatoes contain less starch than rice, peas, or lentils. Condiments added such as butter, sour cream, etc., are the culprits.

As a complex carbohydrate, potatoes are digested more slowly than sugars, yielding energy over a longer period of time. A potato supplies an appreciable amount of vitamin B (riboflavin, thiamine, and niacin). Also, one medium potato furnishes 1/3 of the vitamin C recommended daily for the average adult. It is a good source of fiber.

There are numerous varieties of potatoes but the green grocer will probably have only three or four types. Many markets identify them simply as baking, boiling, or all-purpose.

From the culinary point of view, potatoes can be identified as two basic types: thick-skinned and thin-skinned. The thick-skinned, the longer, oval-shaped variety, which is mealy textured, adapts best for baking, mashing, and French-frying. These mealy varieties tend to fall apart when boiled. The russet potato is one of the favorites for baking and French-fries; it contains less water than some other varieties, and the high solid content makes French-fries stay crisp longer and have a fluffier interior.

The thin-skinned, long whites, round whites, and round reds, which are harder and waxier, are best suited for boiling, steaming, and other uses. These varieties will not be fluffy when baked, and they will be somewhat gluey when mashed.

The term "new potatoes" refers to potatoes (usually the round variety, white- or red-skinned) that are dug young and shipped directly from harvest to market.

In recipes, unless a particular kind is specified, any type of potato may be used.

Varieties

Russet or Idaho: A large, oblong potato with rough brown skin, the russet has a high starch content and little moisture, making it ideal for baking; the potato comes out fluffy and dry. It's also good mashed or French-fried.

Round red: The round red is small with smooth reddish skin and a high moisture content that gives it a waxy appearance. It's excellent when boiled or steamed in its skin.

Round white or Irish: While similar to the round red in shape, the round white has a beige skin. It is a boiling potato, also good for roasting and mashing.

Long white: The same color as the round white, the long white is oblong like the russet. It is an all-purpose potato.

Buying and Storing Potatoes

When choosing potatoes, look for firm, heavy, evenly shaped ones without cuts, bruises, or sprouts. Do not buy potatoes with greenish tinge, a result of overexposure to light.

Avoid storing potatoes in refrigerator because at temperatures below 40 degrees the consistency and taste change; the starch converts to sugar. And do not store potatoes with onions; they both emit

gases which shortens shelf life of both. They'll stay fresh and firm longer if they are stored in a bag along with an apple. The apple gives off a gas that prevents potatoes from sprouting.

Store potatoes in a dark, cool, unrefrigerated place. Forty five to 50 degrees is ideal; but potatoes stored even at 70 degrees should keep for many weeks. Carefully remove any green spots, "eyes" or sprouts before using. (Light turns potatoes green, and this green area, like sprouts, is poisonous and should be cut off and discarded.)

New Potatoes in Their Jackets

Scrub the small potatoes with a vegetable brush and wash in cold running water. Place in saucepan and cook in boiling salted water, covered, about 20 minutes until tender. Drain; and holding saucepan over heat, dry potatoes for a minute; add butter and desired seasonings; toss potatoes to gently coat. Liberally buttered boiled potatoes in their jackets compliment any meal. Allow 2 or 3 small potatoes for a serving.

Parsley Buttered Potatoes

Choose small boiling potatoes of uniform size. Scrape, wash and cook in about 1-inch boiling salted water; cover; cook until tender when tested. Whole potatoes will take about 20 minutes; cut up, a shorter time. Drain thoroughly and hold over heat a few seconds to evaporate excess moisture; add some butter and gently shake skillet to coat the potatoes. Pour into heated serving dish and sprinkle with chopped fresh parsley; serve immediately.

Creamed New Potatoes and Peas

12 small new potatoes	10-ounce package frozen peas
3 tablespoons butter	1 teaspoon onion powder
3 tablespoons flour	2 cups rich milk or half and half
Salt and pepper to taste	

Scrape potatoes under running water; cook in small amount of boiling water slightly salted; drain; keep warm. Meanwhile cook peas following package instructions; drain. Melt butter; stir in flour and seasonings; gradually stir in milk; cook, stirring, until sauce is smooth and thickened. Add potatoes and peas; heat through. Pour into hot serving dish. Top with a little butter. Serves 6.

Mashed Potatoes

Plan on about 1/4 cup milk, 1 teaspoon butter, and salt and pepper to taste for each medium-sized potato used. And adding a little onion powder, if desired, enhances the flavor.

Pare and cut into quarters; boil the potatoes until tender. Drain; pan dry. Pour into heated mixer bowl; beat; add butter and beat hard. Slowly add scalded milk and seasonings, beating continually, until desired consistency. Continue to beat until fluffy as a soufflé. Adjust seasonings; pile lightly into hot serving dish and serve with a spoonful of butter in center.

Scalloped Potatoes

8 medium potatoes	2 cups rich milk or half and half
1 teaspoon onion powder	Salt and pepper to taste
1 tablespoon flour	1/4 teaspoon chicken bouillon

Peel potatoes; slice thin. Blend a little milk into flour to make smooth; then blend in milk and seasonings, stirring, cook until smooth; adjust seasonings; add potatoes and again bring to a boil. Pour into well-buttered 2-quart casserole. Bake at 325 degrees until potatoes are tender, 30 to 40 minutes. Makes 6 to 8 servings. For variations: top with partially cooked bacon pieces or top with grated cheese to bake. Or add sliced frankfurters, diced celery, chipped beef, or grated carrots.

Baked Potatoes

Russets are a favorite for baking. Choose potatoes of uniform size. Scrub potatoes under cold running water. Dry thoroughly with paper towels. Pierce skins with small skewer so skins will not burst while baking. (Brush with salad oil or bacon grease if you like skins soft after baking.) Place on baking sheet or oven rack and bake about 1 hour until tender when tested with a fork or feel soft when squeezed. Although 400 degrees is the optimum baking temperature, if oven is set for another dish, bake potatoes along with it until tender.

Bake potatoes wrapped in foil when you wish to hold them after baking; they will have soft tender skins; but don't expect them to be fluffy. They will be more like a steamed potato.

To serve, slash an X in top of each potato. Then holding potato with pot holder, squeeze ends so steam can escape and potato puffs

up. Add a pat of butter; sprinkle with salt and pepper. Or serve a relish container with whipped butter, dairy sour cream, crisp bacon pieces, or chopped green onions and let everyone top own potato. Let each guest determine number of calories to add!

To Bake in Microwave Oven

Follow manufacturer's directions for baking potatoes, but keep in mind the texture will not be the same as a potato baked in a regular oven. For crisp-skinned, fluffy baked potatoes, the standard oven is still your best bet. But cooking for one, timewise the microwave is a great saving.

Roasted Potatoes

Scrape potatoes clean, dry well, and then wrap a strip of bacon around each potato. Add a little chopped onion to each; wrap individually in foil, then roast.

Left-Over Boiled, Mashed, or Baked Potatoes

Make patties out of mashed potatoes; season as desired and sauté in butter until lightly browned on either side. Nice served with bacon and eggs.

Peeled, baked potatoes and boiled potatoes with jackets are ideal for salads, pan fried in butter, or creamed. To cream, heat some butter and cream in a skillet; add the peeled, sliced, cooked potatoes; season with salt, pepper, and onion powder. Simmer until heated through and creamy thickness desired. These can be heated quickly in a dish in the microwave oven.

Hot Potato Salad

I never cared for potato salad, but when *Better Homes And Gardens* had a Hot Potato Salad contest, I decided to check a bunch of recipes I'd collected. I picked out items I thought best and made up a recipe and sent copy to enter contest. I came in third.

6 slices bacon	1/4 cup chopped onion
1 tablespoon all-purpose flour	1 tablespoon sugar
1/2 teaspoon salt	1/2 teaspoon celery seed
Dash pepper	1/3 cup vinegar
1/4 cup water	1/4 cup mayonnaise or salad dressing
2 hard-cooked eggs, chopped	1 tablespoon snipped parsley
4 cups cooked diced potatoes	

Cook bacon till crisp; drain, reserving 2 tablespoons drippings. Add onion to reserved bacon drippings in skillet; cook till tender but not brown. Blend in flour, sugar, salt, celery seed, and pepper. Stir in vinegar and water; cook and stir until boiling. Remove from heat; stir in mayonnaise, chopped eggs, and parsley. Crumble in bacon. Pour over potatoes; toss to coat. Spoon into a 1-quart casserole. Bake in moderate oven (350) 20 minutes or till heated through. Serves 6.

Squash

The squash family is as varied as it is colorful; each year new varieties of squash are introduced; some have soft shells, some have hard, and some are firm but not hard; and sizes vary as much as shells. But one thing they all have in common is food value. Nutritionally, all varieties are high in fiber and low in calories and sodium. They are also good sources of Vitamin C, niacin, phosphorus, and potassium. And the yellow-fleshed winter squash are high in Vitamin A. The deeper the golden or orange hue, the more the vitamin A it contains. If counting calories, keep in mind that a helping of winter squash has about 1/3 the calorie count of a comparable potion of sweet potato or yam.

There are two distinct types of squash—summer and winter. Summer squash are the quick-growing varieties with soft shells harvested before rinds and seeds begin to harden, such as pattypan, zucchini, and yellow crookneck. They should be refrigerated when purchased and eaten within a few days; they are not good keepers. Winter squash are the late-growing varieties with hard shells and mature seeds, such as acorn, butternut, Hubbard, and kabocha. Winter squash can usually be kept 3 to 6 months in a cool dry place. If cut, wrap in plastic bag and store in refrigerator crisper.

Most varieties within the two categories—summer and winter—are interchangeable in recipes. So experiment to see which you like the best.

Most squash seeds are edible. Larger ones, like pumpkin seeds, can be toasted. And all squash blossoms are edible. The baby zucchini and crooknecks can be served with the smaller female blossoms still attached, while the larger male ones (which do not bear

fruit) can be stuffed or sliced into ribbons and tossed with pasta. Once there is a swelling at the base of the blossom, indicating that the squash has set, the flower can be picked without damage to the squash. For larger flowers for stuffing, just wait until the blossoms drop naturally from the plant. Of course, don't expect to purchase squash with their blossoms on at the market—that is a reward of the home gardener.

Yellow Crookneck and Yellow Straightneck

The crookneck squash curves at the neck, is larger at tip than at base and has a thin, moderately warted skin, which is light yellow and edible when immature; the flesh is creamy yellow, rather fine. It grows to 8- to 10-inches long and about 2 1/2- to 3-inches in diameter. There are also larger crooknecks.

The yellow straightneck is same as yellow crookneck, but is relatively straight, with a smooth skin.

Both squash turn a deeper yellow as they mature. Both are available throughout the year. They do not store well.

To cook: Allow 2 pounds for 4 servings.

When ready to cook, wash and scrub well with a brush; cut off stem and blossom ends, but not peel. Slice or dice. Cook, covered, in a very small amount of boiling salted water until tender, 15 to 20 minutes. Drain; mash; add butter, salt and seasoned pepper to taste, and enough cream for desired smoothness.

Zucchini

Zucchini is a shiny dark green, straight-sided cylindrical squash, which is at its best eating stage when 6- to 8-inches long. The flesh is creamy white and tender.

"Plain" Summer Squash

Zucchini, Pattypan or Scallop, and Yellow Crookneck cooked individually or all three together are simply delicious the quick and easy way. Wash squash but do not peel; cut off blossom and stem ends; cut into 1/2-inch slices. Cook, covered, in very small amount of boiling water seasoned with salt, sugar, chicken bouillon, and a little butter until just tender. The liquid should be practically evaporated. Be careful not to burn.

Zucchetta Rampicanti

This Italian zucchini squash is most unusual; the long, curled, slender, pale green squash has a bulge in the blossom end where the seeds are contained. It is a wonderfully flavored zucchini; this serpent-like squash has an unusual, sweet, subtle flavor and can be eaten like a raw apple.

Zucchini with Baby Carrots

3/4 pound baby carrots	1/8 teaspoon black pepper
2 medium zucchini	1/4 teaspoon chicken stock base
1/3 cup water	1/4 teaspoon onion powder
1 tablespoon butter	1/4 teaspoon sugar

Scrape carrots; cut zucchini diagonally into 1/2-inch slices. Combine all ingredients except zucchini in a large non-stick skillet. Cover and cook about 5 minutes, stirring occasionally. Add zucchini; cover and cook over high heat, stirring a couple times, until vegetables are crisp-tender and liquid absorbed. Adjust seasonings. Serves 4.

Shredded Zucchini with Onions

1 pound zucchini	1 tablespoon butter
1 medium onion	1/2 teaspoon brown sugar
Salt and pepper to taste	1/4 teaspoon chicken bouillon

Coarsely grate zucchini. Peel and mince onion. In heavy skillet over moderate heat, cook onions, covered, about 3 minutes until transparent. Add zucchini; cook and stir until zucchini is crispy tender. Stir in seasonings to taste.

"Zucchini Combo" (Microwave) Excellent!

3 cups sliced zucchini	1 teaspoon onion powder
2 tablespoons butter	1/4 cup grated Parmesan cheese
2 medium tomatoes	Salt and pepper to taste

Slice and layer zucchini in 1 1/2-quart casserole. Add onion powder and butter. Cover and microwave about 7 minutes, stirring once during that time. Slice and quarter tomatoes; spread over zucchini; sprinkle on cheese. Microwave 1 to 2 minutes until cheese has melted. Salt and pepper to taste.

Oven-Fried Zucchini Stick

1/2 cup Miracle Whip®	4 4- to 6-ounce size zucchini
Pinch of sugar	1 cup fine cracker crumbs
Salt and pepper to taste	1/4 teaspoon onion powder

Slice zucchini into quarters lengthwise. Combine seasonings and cracker crumbs. Spread Miracle Whip® on all sides of zucchini sticks; roll in seasoned cracker crumbs. Place on ungreased non-stick baking sheet. Bake at 350 to 400 degrees until golden brown, about 20 minutes. Turn, if necessary, for even browning.

Zucchini Pancakes

2 eggs, lightly beaten	2 cups grated unpeeled zucchini
1/2 cup milk	1 cup pancake mix
1/4 teaspoon salt	1/4 teaspoon onion powder (optional)
2 teaspoons brown sugar	

Beat egg and milk together; stir in remaining ingredients. Heat heavy non-stick griddle on medium heat. Using a 1/4-cup measure, pour mixture onto hot surface and cook until golden brown, turn and brown other side. Stir batter and continue until all batter has been used, brushing griddle with a little butter, if necessary. Makes 8 to 10 four-inch pancakes.

Zucchini Stuffed Quiche

4 eggs	4 cups shredded zucchini
1/2 teaspoon sugar	2 tablespoons chopped parsley
1 teaspoon flour	1/2 teaspoon chicken bouillon
1 1/3 cups rich milk	4 ounces shredded Swiss cheese
8 thin slices bacon	1/2 teaspoon onion powder
Salt and pepper to taste	

Use either sautéed bacon or 2 cups shredded ham. If bacon, sauté slices but not crisp; squeeze in paper towel to remove grease; then shred. Generously butter a 9-inch pie plate or 6 individual 10-ounce casseroles. Combine zucchini, chicken bouillon, onion powder, sugar, and 1/4 teaspoon salt together; press into buttered pie plate or casseroles to make a crust. Sprinkle grated cheese over top; top with shredded cooked bacon or ham. Beat together eggs, flour, salt and seasoned pepper to taste. Stir in milk and parsley; pour over ingredients in crust. Bake at 400 degrees about 20 minutes until custard is set.

Acorn Squash (Also called Table Queen or Danish)

Acorn squash is really a miniature version of a Hubbard. It is acorn-shaped with a hard, thin, deeply-furrowed, green to yellow-gold shell, with slightly dry, sweet tasting, yellowish flesh.

It is the perfect size for halving and stuffing. It can also be sliced into rings and baked or steamed; and is excellent to mash (because it does not become watery) or purée and serve simply with herbs, spices, butter, nuts, or a little cream. Or it is delicious puréed and combined with equal amounts of mashed potatoes, sweet potatoes, rutabagas, or turnips.

Baked Acorn Squash

Ideal-sized acorn is large enough for 2 servings. Cut in half; scoop out seeds and membrane; sprinkle cavity with brown sugar and about 1 teaspoon butter. Set on baking sheet; bake in 350- to 375-degree oven 45 to 55 minutes.

If desired, remove baked pulp from shell; mash; season with butter, salt and seasoned pepper; refill shells; heat and serve.

Or bake whole, (pierced), at 375 degrees 45 to 55 minutes. Cut in half; remove seeds and membrane. Remove pulp; mash; add butter; season to taste. Serve hot.

Acorn Squash Meal in One

2 acorn squash	1 pound lean ground beef
1/2 cup chopped onion	1/4 cup fine cracker crumbs
1/2 cup chopped celery	2/3 cup evaporated milk
Salt and pepper to taste	2 teaspoons brown sugar, optional

Cut squash in halves lengthwise. Remove seeds and membrane. Place cut-side up on rack in a 13- by 9-inch baking pan. Pour in 1/2-inch water in bottom of pan. Bake at 350 degrees 40 minutes.

Sprinkle 1/2 teaspoon brown sugar into each squash half, if desired. Combine ground beef, cracker crumbs, seasonings, celery,

onions, and milk; mix lightly but thoroughly. Divide into fourths; shape into balls; place in squash cavities. Return to oven and bake at 350 degrees about 40 minutes until meat is done. (Or bake at 400 degrees about 20 minutes.)

Tomatoes

Is the tomato a fruit or vegetable? This was the question that led to one of the most unusual legal battles in American history. And it took the U.S. Supreme Court two weeks to decide the issue.

Controversy over the tomato started in 1886 when the firm of Nix, Nix, and Nix had to pay an import tax on a cargo of tomatoes from Bermuda.

Under the tariff act passed three years earlier, there was a tax on vegetables but not a tax on fruits. And the customs collector said that tomatoes were vegetables, therefore subject to tax.

The Nix firm argued that tomatoes were fruit, but the customs collector refused to yield.

The importers paid the tax rather than lose their cargo, but they didn't let the matter rest. They were intent on getting a refund. The only way to do this was to take the matter to court to prove legally that the tomato was a fruit.

Action got under way in the lower courts. The case went to the Circuit Court of the Southern District of New York in 1889, where the custom collector's decision was upheld.

The Nix firm elected to appeal to the highest court of the land. Oddly enough, instead of throwing the case out as ridiculous, the Supreme Court began weighing evidence on the tomato. For two weeks they debated the question: Is the tomato a fruit or a vegetable?

The seven-year argument finally came to a close. On May 10, 1893, the justices ruled: "Botanically speaking, tomatoes are the fruit of a vine, just as are cucumbers, squashes, beans and peas. But in the common language of the people, all these are vegetables ...since they are grown in gardens and are generally used during the main part of a meal. They are unlike fruits which are appetizers or desserts or eaten out of hand," the court declared. So the public's idea of the tomato as a vegetable swayed the court. The Nix firm lost the big fight to classify it as a fruit and did not get its refund. And the court's decision still stands today.

Ripened Tomatoes

Tomatoes are fiber-rich and low in calories, fat, and sodium and contain no cholesterol. There is nothing quite like a thin-skinned, luscious red tomato that has ripened on the vine. The locally vine-ripened (in hothouse or field) are thin-skinned, juicy and flavorful, as well as rich in vitamins C and A, and have potassium, calcium, pllouphorus, and iron.

A tomato ripens on the vine by producing its own ethylene. Commercially shipped tomatoes are usually picked at the "mature green" stage, placed in a ripening room for about 48 hours exposed to ethylene, a hydrocarbon gas, so the tomatoes will burn red and stay firm for shipping. If the tomato was picked when truly mature green, it matches its vine-ripe counterpart in nutrients. Unfortunately, immature green tomatoes are also being picked, and supposedly they are lower in vitamin C and not as sweet.

Contrary to popular belief, tomatoes should not be set to ripen on sunny windowsills. They do better on a counter. If the tomato is still slightly green, the ripening process can be hastened by putting it in a paper bag with an apple; the apple gives off ethylene, the same gas tomatoes naturally produce to ripen themselves.

As soon as a vine-ripened tomato is cut, it releases natural chemicals that give it a pleasing aroma. A scientific test indicates the best way to enjoy the full flavor of a ripe tomato is to eat it at room temperature—and as soon as it has been cut.

Because tomato flavor develops as it ripens on the plant, no tomato that you find in a market will have a flavor as good as one you pick, ripe from the vine. This is because tomatoes allowed to ripen fully before picking would be much too tender to stand mass harvesting, much less shipping. So, unfortunately, growers must aim for the best compromise.

All tomatoes aren't red like those found in the supermarket. They also come in yellow, white, pale yellow, pink-purple, orange, apricot, even striped green; and they come in various sizes.

To Peel Tomatoes

Normally this is done by immersing the tomato into boiling water about a minute then immediately plunging the tomato into cold water. You start peeling at the stem end with a paring knife; the skin will peel off easily. But peeling can be accomplished much more easily in the microwave, one of whose virtues is that it gives off no heat and remains cool. Cook the tomato on HIGH for about 15 seconds; let stand a few seconds and then peel with ease.

Stuffed Cherry Tomatoes

24	cherry tomatoes		3-ounce package chipped beef
1	teaspoon onion powder	1	tablespoon minced celery
1	tablespoon cream		8-ounce package cream cheese
	Chopped parsley	1	teaspoon Worcestershire sauce

Cut out stem end, hollow out tomatoes removing seeds. Season insides with salt and sugar; drain upside down; chill. Cut chipped beef fine; combine ingredients; adjust seasonings; stuff tomatoes. Chill. Serve on tray with stuffed celery sticks, pickles, etc.

Fried Tomatoes, Country Style

Select firm, ripe tomatoes; cut off slice from each end; cut the balance into thick slices. Dust with salt, pepper, flour, and a little sugar.

Crisp fry a couple slices lean bacon; remove from skillet and fry tomato slices in the bacon grease until nicely browned on both sides. Arrange slices on warned serving plate.

Crumble the bacon slices; add to skillet with a cup of rich milk seasoned with onion powder. Heat just to thicken. Pour over tomatoes and garnish with a little chopped parsley. Add a couple drops of Worchestershire sauce, if desired.

Baked Tomato Halves

2	large tomatoes	1	tablespoon minced parsley
1/4	cup cracker crumbs	1	teaspoon onion powder
1	teaspoon sugar		Salt and pepper to taste
1/4	cup Miracle Whip®		

Preheat oven to 400 degrees. Slice tomatoes crosswise in halves. Gently squeeze out seeds and juice; place upside down to drain. Combine remaining ingredients. Set tomato halves cut-side up in buttered custard cups; divide mixture and spread over top of each. Set cups on baking sheet. Bake until golden brown, about 25 minutes. Serve immediately. Makes 4 accompaniment servings.

Tomato Aspic Ring

2 cups tomato juice	2 whole cloves
3 tablespoons sliced onion	Small diced carrot
2 tablespoons finely cut celery	1 1/2 tablespoons Knox® gelatin
1 tablespoon lemon juice	1 tablespoon brown sugar
Shredded lettuce	1/4 teaspoon salt
2 hard-cooked eggs, sliced	1 small bay leaf
Sliced black olives	

Combine 1 1/2 cups tomato juice, bay leaf, carrot, onion, celery, salt and cloves; bring to a boil and simmer 5 minutes. Strain in coarse sieve; discard pulp.

Soften gelatin in the 1/2 cup chilled tomato juice; stir into hot mixture; add lemon juice. Chill until partially set; then pour into slightly greased individual ring molds or a large ring mold. Chill until firm.

On the service plate or individual salad plates, scatter shredded greens. Unmold the aspic on the greens and surround with sliced egg and sliced black olives. Place 1/2 tablespoon of Miracle Whip® salad dressing in center of each aspic.

Or fill center of ring with combination of chilled tuna, diced celery, and mayonnaise. Garnish with a sprig of parsley or watercress in center. Serves 6.

Tomato Sauce, Tomato Purée, and Tomato Paste

The tomato is the common base for these three, but the preparation for each is different.

Tomato puree is the preparation obtained by forcing the tomato through a sieve to separate the flesh from the seeds and peel; then cooking the sieved results to reduce it to thickish consistency. Properly, tomato purée is unseasoned.

Tomato sauce is tomato purée seasoned and combined with other ingredients.

Tomato paste is very concentrated purée, frequently made with plum tomatoes, always seasoned.

Fresh Tomato Purée

Peel, seed, and chop 2 ripe tomatoes and combine them in a

nonstick saucepan. Cook them, stirring frequently until tomatoes are reduced to a pulp. Strain the pulp through a fine sieve and season the purée with salt and pepper to taste.

Tomato Pulp

A pound of tomatoes, peeled and seeded, will yield about one cup pulp.

Tomato Soufflé

Coat a 2-quart oven-proof dish (or six 20-ounce dishes) with butter. Sprinkle with fine Ritz® cracker crumbs to coat. Set aside.

3 tablespoons butter	3 eggs, separated
1/4 teaspoon salt (or to taste)	1/4 cup flour
1/4 teaspoon brown sugar	Sprinkle of white pepper
1/4 teaspoon chili powder	1 cup condensed tomato soup
1/4 pound sharp Cheddar cheese, grated	1/2 teaspoon ground dry mustard
	1 teaspoon cream of tartar

Place flour in a small saucepan; stir in tomato soup until well blended; add the butter, salt and sugar; set over medium heat; cook about 3 minutes, stirring constantly, until thickened. Remove from heat; stir in cheese and remaining spices; beat until smooth. Beat in egg yolks until smooth.

Be sure egg whites are at room temperature. Beat egg whites with cream of tartar in a large bowl at high speed until stiffly beaten. Gently fold into tomato mixture.

Pour mixture into prepared soufflé dish (or the individual dishes). Bake on lower shelf of a 325-degree preheated oven until puffed and deep golden. Less time for individuals. Serve immediately.

Cookies

Helpful Hints for Successful Cookie Baking

To measure dry ingredients, use individual dry measuring cups sold in sets of graduated sizes—1 cup, 1/2 cup, 1/3 cup, and 1/4 cup—metal or plastic. To measure flour, stir it a bit right in the package, then gently spoon into exact-size cup until overflowing. Level off with spatula or knife. Be careful not to shake up, tap on counter, or otherwise pack down flour. For nuts, coconut, or cut-up or small fruit, spoon into cup and pack down lightly. For brown sugar, fats, and solid shortening, pack down firmly in right-sized cup.

To measure liquids, pour into glass measuring cup and read measurement at eye level.

Use large eggs in all recipes.

Use stick butter only, not whipped or tub type.

Keep an oven thermometer in your oven to check temperature. Adjust setting if necessary.

Use cookie sheets at least 2 inches narrower and shorter than your oven for proper heat circulation.

Always place dough on a cool cookie sheet (dough spreads on a hot one).

Bake on 1 cookie sheet at a time, in upper 1/3 of oven unless recipe states otherwise. But fill another sheet while the first is in the oven.

Check cookies at the minimum baking time. One minute can make a difference. More important than specified time is how a cookie looks, feels, and smells. And unless otherwise specified, remove cookies immediately from baking sheet. (Leaving them on still hot sheets for even a moment means cookies will keep on baking.) Keep in mind that subsequent batches will bake faster because of oven's heat buildup. Adjust timing accordingly.

If you have problems with your drop cookies being uniformly round, try chilling your dough first. Rather than dropping the mixture onto baking sheet with aid of two teaspoons, roll each teaspoonful of chilled dough between palms of hands. If dough sticks somewhat to hands, drop into a little sifted powdered sugar then roll. Place balls 2 inches apart on chilled or cool non-stick baking sheet. Press balls with finger tips or drinking glass bottom to form flat rounds.

Your cookie dough will roll out, cut out, and transfer to the cookie sheet more easily if you roll it on a lightly floured pastry cloth. In addition, cover your rolling pin with a cloth pastry sleeve and flour it well to minimize sticking as you roll.

Before cutting the cookie dough into shapes, dip your cutters into flour. Use long thin spatula to lift the cutouts from the pastry cloth to your cookie sheet. There is less chance of distorting the shape of the cookies.

When you reroll dough scraps, dust the pastry cloth with a half-and-half-mixture of flour and powdered sugar. This makes the cookies more tender than if they were rerolled on a surface dusted with flour alone.

To Preserve Cookies

Cool cookies completely before storing them in an airtight container to maintain best possible texture. Store soft cookies in one container; crisp cookies in one container (otherwise soft cookies will soften crisp cookies). If storing cookies for more than a few days, consider freezing them. Cookies freeze well and can be stored this way for months, if wrapped airtight to prevent drying and freezer burn.

Delicate Powdered Sugar Cookies

1/2 cup Crisco®	2 1/4 cups sifted flour
1/2 cup butter	1/4 cup cornstarch
1 teaspoon soda	1 1/2 cups sifted powdered sugar
1/4 teaspoon salt	1 teaspoon cream of tartar
1 egg	1 cup chopped pecans, optional
1 teaspoon vanilla	1/4 teaspoon almond extract

Cream shortenings, sugar, egg, and flavorings until light. Stir in sifted dry ingredients. Drop batter by teaspoonful onto ungreased baking sheet. Bake in a 375-degree oven until lightly browned, 8 to 10 minutes. (Dough may be formed into rolls and wrapped in foil; then frozen for future use. Then slice 1/6- to 1/4-inch thick and bake on ungreased baking sheet at 350 degrees about 10 minutes.) Makes 6 dozen crisp cookies.

Famous Oatmeal Cookies

3/4	cup Crisco®	3	cups Quaker® Oats (quick or old
1	cup brown sugar		fashioned, uncooked)
1	cup all-purpose flour	1/2	cup granulated sugar
1/2	teaspoon soda	1/2	teaspoon salt
1	egg	1	teaspoon vanilla
1/4	cup water		

Beat together Crisco®, sugars, egg, water, and vanilla until creamy. Add combined remaining ingredients; mix well. Drop by rounded teaspoonfuls onto greased cookie sheet. Bake in 350-degree oven for 12 to 15 minutes. (For variety, add chopped nuts, raisins, chocolate chips, or coconut.) Makes about 5 dozen cookies.

For variety: Make ice cream sandwich cookies. Drop dough by rounded teaspoonfuls onto greased cookie sheet. Flatten with bottom of 1/2-cup dry measure dipped in granulated sugar. Bake 8 or 9 minutes or until light golden brown. Immediately remove from cooky sheet; cool on wire cooling rack. Spread 2 tablespoonfuls softened ice cream on bottom side of one cooky and top with second. Freeze on tray, continuing until all are made and frozen. When completely frozen, wrap airtight in plastic wrap. Keep frozen until ready to serve.

Toll House® Chocolate-Chip Cookies

The original recipe for Toll House® Cookies was the creation of Ruth Wakefield, who ran a very popular Toll House Restaurant in Massachusetts in the twenties and early thirties. One day Wakefield decided to make chocolate cookies using her butter cookie recipe. Rather than melt the chocolate, she decided to add small pieces of semi-sweet chocolate to the batter. To her surprise, the bits of chocolate didn't dissolve into the batter when the cookie baked and instead of a chocolate cookie, she had a butter cookie with chocolate chips. The cookie was such a success that a few years later she sold the rights to the company that release the bits. And the popularity grew. Now there are innumerable versions of the chocolate-chip cookies.

Quick and Easy Favorite Cocoa Drop Cookies

1/2 cup Crisco	1 1/3 cups sifted flour
1 cup brown sugar	3 teaspoons baking powder
1/2 cup cocoa	1/4 teaspoon salt
2/3 cup milk	1/2 cup chopped nuts or raisins
1 egg	1 teaspoon vanilla

Blend as for any cookie mixture. Drop by teaspoonfuls onto baking sheet. Bake in 400-degree oven until finger lightly pressed in center does not leave an impression. Frost, if desired. Nice with a powdered sugar frosting, sprinkled with chopped nuts.

Fantastic Chocolate Cookies

1/2 cup butter, softened	2 ounces semi-sweet chocolate, melted
1 cup brown sugar	
2 eggs, slightly beaten	1 1/2 cups all-purpose flour
1/2 cup buttermilk	1 teaspoon baking powder
1 teaspoon vanilla	1/2 cup chopped pecans
1/4 teaspoon salt	1/4 teaspoon soda

Mix batter ingredients and drop by teaspoonfuls onto greased baking sheet. Bake at 325 degrees about 10 minutes until finger lightly touched will not leave and impression. Frost cookies while still warm from the oven.

Frosting

1 1/2 tablespoons cocoa	1 1/2 cups sifted powdered sugar
2 tablespoons butter	Enough evaporated milk to
1 teaspoon vanilla	make spreadable

Beat ingredients until smooth and creamy.

Chocolate-Marshmallow Drops

1/2 cup Crisco®	1/2 cup milk
1 cup sugar	1 3/4 cup sifted flour
1/2 cup cocoa	1/2 teaspoon baking soda
1 egg	1/2 cup chopped nuts
1 teaspoon vanilla	24 large marshmallows, cut in half

Cream Crisco®, sugar, pinch of salt, egg, and vanilla until light. Add sifted dry ingredients and milk; mix well. Stir in chopped nuts. Drop by teaspoonsful onto nonstick cookie sheet. Bake in upper one-third of 375-degree oven for 10 minutes; remove from oven; lightly press a marshmallow half, cut side down, on top of each cooky. Return to oven for about 2 minutes until cookies are done and marshmallows are softened. Cool; then cover with Cocoa Glaze. Makes 4 dozen.

Cocoa Glaze
Sift together 2 cups powdered sugar, 1/2 cups cocoa; gradually stir in 4 to 6 tablespoons hot milk to consistency that mixture will spread easily.

Cocoa Kisses

3 egg whites	1/8 teaspoon cream of tartar
1/2 cup sugar	3 tablespoons unsweetened
1 tablespoon cornstarch	cocoa powder
1/4 cup finely chopped pecans	

Have egg whites at room temperature. Beat whites at medium speed until foamy. Add cream of tartar and continue beating until soft peaks form. Add 1/4 cup sugar 1 tablespoon at a time; beat until egg whites are stiff but not dry.

Sift cocoa, cornstarch, and remaining 1/4 cup sugar together. Sprinkle half of mixture over whites; using rubber spatula, gently fold in just until blended. Repeat, folding in remaining cocoa mixture; fold in pecans.

Drop by teaspoonfuls onto two lightly greased baking sheets and position on rack in upper third of 325-degree oven. Bake cookies until set, about 35 minutes. Cool slightly. Using spatula, gently transfer cookies to racks to cool completely.

Elsie Glow's Chocolate Kisses

3 egg whites	6 ounces chocolate chips
1 cup powdered sugar	1/2 cup graham cracker crumbs
1 teaspoon vanilla	1/2 cup chopped pecans

Melt chocolate in top of double boiler; cool. Beat egg whites until stiff but not dry. Beat in sugar about 2 tablespoons at a time. Fold in

cracker crumbs, pecans, and vanilla. Gently fold in chocolate. Drop by teaspoonfuls onto buttered cookie sheet. Bake in 350-degree oven for 12 minutes. Makes about 5 dozen.

Mocha Pecan Meringue Kisses

2 large egg whites	1/4 teaspoon cream of tartar
1/2 cup chopped pecans	1/2 cup sifted powdered sugar
1/3 cup semi-sweet chocolate pieces	1/2 teaspoon instant coffee
Pinch of salt	

Beat egg whites, a pinch of salt, and cream of tartar until soft peaks form; gradually add sugar; beat until stiff. Fold in pecans and semi-sweet chocolate pieces. Drop by teaspoonfuls onto lightly greased baking pan. Bake in a 300-degree oven 25 to 30 minutes until lightly browned. Let set 5 minutes, then remove with spatula to cooling rack.

Elegant Chocolate Chip Cookies

1 cup Crisco®	2 cups flour
1 cup brown sugar	2 teaspoons baking powder
1/4 teaspoon salt	1/2 cup granulated sugar
2 eggs	2 cups chocolate chips
1 teaspoon vanilla	1 cup broken nut meats

Cream Crisco® (use half butter and half Crisco®, if desired), eggs, sugars, and vanilla until light. Stir in sifted dry ingredients. Add chocolate chips and nuts; stir just to blend. Drop by teaspoonsful onto nonstick cookie sheet. Bake at 350 degrees on rack in upper third of oven until golden. Makes about 5 dozen.

Gourmet Cookies

1 cup Crisco®	1 teaspoon baking powder
1/2 cup granulated sugar	1 teaspoon soda
7/8 cup brown sugar	1/2 teaspoon salt
2 extra-large eggs	2 cups sugar-coated cornflakes
2 teaspoons vanilla	2 cups Quaker Oats®
1 cup raisins	1 cup chocolate chips
2 cups flour	1 cup finely chopped pecans

Cream Crisco®, sugars, salt, eggs, and vanilla until light. Sift together flour, baking powder, and soda; then sift dry ingredients into creamed mixture; mix well. Blend in oats, cornflakes, chips, raisins, and pecans; mix well. On nonstick cookie sheet, drop rounded teaspoonfuls 1 inch apart. Bake in upper one-third of 350-degree oven about 15 minutes until light golden brown. Makes about 7 dozen.

Chunky White Chocolate Macadamia Nut Cookies

1/2 cup butter, softened	2 cups all-purpose flour
1/2 cup Crisco®	1/2 teaspoon baking powder
1 large egg	8 ounces white chocolate chips
3/4 cup brown sugar	2 tablespoons granulated sugar
1/8 teaspoon salt	7 ounces salted whole
3/4 teaspoon soda	macadamia nuts
1 1/2 teaspoons vanilla extract	

Beat together butter, Crisco®, sugars, egg, and vanilla until light. Beat in dry ingredients; stir in white chocolate chips and nuts; stir until evenly distributed. Drop dough in rounded teaspoonfuls onto greased baking sheets, spacing them 2 1/2 inches apart. Flatten tops of cookies slightly. Bake in center of preheated 375-degree oven until lightly golden, about 9 minutes. Be very careful not to overbake. Remove from oven and let stand 2 to 3 minutes. Using a spatula, transfer cookies to wire racks to cool completely. Makes about 3 dozen 2 3/4-inch cookies.

Old-Fashioned Hermits

1/2 cup Crisco®	2 cups all-purpose flour
1/2 cup granulated sugar	2 teaspoons baking powder
1/2 cup brown sugar	1 teaspoon cinnamon
2 eggs	1/2 teaspoon nutmeg
1 cup golden raisins	1/4 teaspoon cloves
3/4 cup chopped walnuts	1/4 teaspoon salt

Thoroughly beat shortening, sugars, and eggs together. Blend in sifted dry ingredients. Add raisins and walnuts; mix well. Drop by teaspoonfuls onto greased baking sheet. Bake at 350 degrees 12 to 15 minutes or until lightly browned. Makes about 3 dozen cookies.

Krumkake (Pronounced "kroom-kocka")

4 eggs, separated	1 1/2 cups flour
1 cup sugar	2 tablespoons cornstarch
1 teaspoon vanilla	1/2 cup butter, softened

Cream butter, sugar, egg yolks, and vanilla; stir in sifted flour and cornstarch. Fold in beaten egg whites. Drop by tablespoon on center of hot krumkake griddle. Bake until delicately browned. Remove from iron with a spatula or table knife. Roll quickly on cone or shape over glass to form baskets. Krumkake should be kept in an airtight, dry container to retain crispness.

Pepparkakor (Swedish spice cake)

1 cup butter	3 1/4 cup sifted all-purpose flour
1 1/2 cups brown sugar	2 teaspoons baking soda
2 teaspoons grated orange peel	2 teaspoons cinnamon
2 tablespoons dark corn syrup	1/2 teaspoon cloves
1 tablespoon warm water	

Beat butter and 1 1/2 cups sugar in mixing bowl. Add egg and beat until light and fluffy. Stir in orange peel, corn syrup, and water; blend well. Sift flour, baking soda, and spices into medium bowl, then stir into beaten mixture. Wrap and refrigerate 4 hours or overnight.

Preheat oven to 375 degrees. Roll a small amount of dough 1/8 inch thick on lightly floured surface. Keep remaining dough refrigerated until ready to roll. Cut rolled dough into desired shapes. Place on ungreased cookie sheets. Bake 8 to 10 minutes. Transfer to wire racks to cool completely.

Fabulous Coconut Macaroons

3 egg whites	2 tablespoons cornstarch
1 cup sugar	3 cups shredded coconut
Dash of salt	1 teaspoon vanilla

Beat egg whites until stiff but not dry; beat in sugar. Fold in shredded coconut and cornstarch. Cook in top of double boiler 15 minutes, stirring continually. Add vanilla; drop by teaspoonfuls onto greased baking sheet. Bake about 25 minutes in 300-degree oven until delicate brown. Remove from baking sheet while warm.

Date Shaggies (Crisp, crunchy—really good!)

1/4 cup butter	1 cup all-purpose flour
1/4 cup Crisco®	1/4 teaspoon baking soda
1/4 teaspoon salt	1/4 cup granulated sugar
1/2 cup brown sugar	1 cup chopped dates
1 large egg	1/2 cup pecans, chopped
1 teaspoon vanilla	2 1/2 cups sugar-frosted flakes

Spoon 2 tablespoons of the sifted dry ingredients over nuts and dates so dates do not stick together. Beat butter, Crisco®, egg, sugars, and vanilla until light. Stir in sifted flour; stir in nut-date mixture. Chill dough. Slightly crush sugar-frosted corn flakes. Roll dough by half teaspoonfuls in crushed flakes, coating well. Place two inches apart on non-stick cookie sheet. Bake on rack in upper one-third of a 375-degree oven until slightly browned, about 12 minutes. Makes about 3 dozen cookies.

Heavenly Christmas Rocks

1/2 cup Crisco®	2 1/2 cups sifted flour, divided
1/2 cup butter	1 teaspoon baking powder
1 1/2 cups brown sugar	1 teaspoon soda
3 eggs	2 cups cut-up candied cherries
1 teaspoon cinnamon	2 cups cut-up candied pineapple
1 1/2 teaspoons vanilla	1 cup blanched almonds, sliced
1/2 teaspoon salt	1 cup Brazil nuts, sliced
2 cups cut-up dates	1 cup pecans, sliced

Toss fruit and nuts with 1/2 cup of the flour. Beat together sugar, butter, Crisco®, eggs, and vanilla until very light. Stir in sifted dry ingredients; blend thoroughly. Add fruit and nuts and mix thoroughly. Drop by teaspoonfuls onto nonstick cookie sheet. Bake in upper 1/3 of oven at 325 degrees until golden, 18 to 20 minutes. Makes about 12 dozen wonderful cookies. These are good keepers; they freeze nicely.

Mexican Wedding Cookies

1/2 cup butter	1 3/4 cups sifted all-purpose flour
1/2 cup Crisco®	1 cup finely chopped pecans
1/2 cup powdered sugar	1 1/4 teaspoons vanilla extract
1/4 teaspoon salt	1/2 teaspoon almond extract
	2/3 cup powdered sugar

Cream butter, Crisco®, and 1/2 cup powdered sugar in large bowl. Stir in flavorings. Mix in sifted flour and salt; stir in pecans; stir until smooth. Chill mixture until firm, about 1 hour. Form dough into 1-inch balls and place on baking sheet, spacing evenly. Bake on center rack in preheated 300-degree oven until light golden brown, about 35 minutes. Transfer to rack and cool. Place 2/3 cup powdered sugar in medium bowl; roll cookies in sugar to coat completely. Cool. Store in airtight container at room temperature. Reroll in sugar before serving.

Pecan Balls

1/2 cup butter	1 cup finely chopped pecans
1/4 cup powdered sugar	1 teaspoon vanilla
1 cup sifted flour	2 tablespoons cocoa, optional
Pinch of salt	Powdered sugar for rolling

Mix ingredients; chill until firm enough to handle. Roll dough a teaspoonful at a time into marble-sized balls between the palms of hands; place 2 inches apart on ungreased baking sheet. Bake at 325 degrees until lightly golden, about 20 minutes. Cool on baking sheet about 5 minutes; remove carefully. Roll in powdered sugar while still warm to make a generous white coating. Makes 4 dozen.

Mocha–Nut Balls

1 cup butter	2 teaspoons instant coffee
1/2 cup sugar	1/4 teaspoon salt
2 teaspoons vanilla	2 cups finely chopped pecans
1 3/4 cups flour	1/4 cup unsweetened cocoa
Powdered sugar for rolling	

Cream butter, sugar, and vanilla; stir in sifted dry ingredients; then chopped nuts. Chill dough until easy to handle. Shape into 1-inch balls; place on nonstick cookie sheet. Bake in 325-degree oven 15 to 20 minutes. Cool; roll in powdered sugar to coat.

Almond Lace Wafers (Special)

1/4 cup sugar	1 1/2 tablespoons flour
1/4 cup butter	1/3 cup finely chopped blanched
1 tablespoon cream	almonds

Melt butter in small saucepan; stir in remaining ingredients; remove from heat. Drop by teaspoonfuls, 3 inches apart, on well-buttered cookie sheet; spread each into a 2-inch round. Make only 4 to 6 wafers at a time so they do not touch. Bake at 350 degrees 5 to 6 minutes until light golden. Cool on cookie sheet 2 to 3 minutes until firm enough to remove with spatula. Cool completely on wire racks.

Rolled Almond Wafers (Choice)

2 egg whites	1/3 cup sifted flour
1/2 cup sugar	3 tablespoons melted butter
1/3 cup finely chopped almonds	

Beat egg whites until stiff; slowly add the sugar, beating constantly. Carefully fold in flour, melted butter, and blanched finely chopped almonds. Drop by teaspoonfuls, 3 inches apart on well-buttered cookie sheet; spread each into a very thin 2- to 3-inch round. Bake only 5 or 6 at a time so they can be shaped quickly. Bake at 450 degrees 3 to 4 minutes just until golden. Remove each quickly and carefully from cookie sheet with spatula. With fingers, shape at once into a roll; cool on wire rack. Continue to bake and shape cookies, buttering cookie sheet well each time. Sprinkle wafers with powdered sugar. Makes 2 1/2 dozen.

Lacey Oat Wafers (Delightful)

1/3 cup butter	1/2 teaspoon baking powder
2/3 cup brown sugar	1/2 cup chopped pecans
Pinch of salt	1 tablespoon milk
1 cup oats	1/2 teaspoon vanilla

Cream together butter and sugar until light and fluffy. Stir in remaining ingredients, blending well. Drop by teaspoonfuls about 2 inches apart on nonstick baking sheet. Bake at 350 degrees about 8 minutes. Cool 2 to 3 minutes, then remove from baking sheet. If cookies harden before removal from sheet, reheat in oven a few minutes to soften. Cookies will be very thin and lacy. Makes 2 1/2 dozen. (Note: If cookies are to be rolled into cornucopias, they must be very warm. Do this one by one as they are removed from baking sheet.)

Fortune Cookies (Made on griddle)

For fortunes, rely on your own wit or books of poetry or proverbs. Original messages are good way to provide entertainment; fate has a curious way of matching appropriate fortunes and people. Write fortunes first, then cut the paper into 1/2- by 3-inch strips. And have cotton gloves to handle hot cooky quickly and a muffin pan on hand to hold the folded cooky in shape for a few minutes.

The following two recipes are not authentic recipes (but then cookies you get in restaurants aren't authentic Chinese, either). These are larger and more delicate.

1 egg white	1 tablespoon cornstarch
2 tablespoons sugar	2 tablespoons cooking oil
Dash of salt	1/4 cup cake flour
1 tablespoon water	

Add sifted dry ingredients to oil and egg white; beat until smooth; add water; mix well. Make one cookie at a time. Pour 1 tablespoonful of batter onto lightly greased griddle, spreading batter to 3 1/2-inch circle. Cook over low heat about 4 minutes until lightly browned. With wide spatula, lift and turn; cook 1 minute more. Working quickly, place cookie on pot holder, put fortune in center; fold cookie in half to form a semi-circle. Fold again over edge of bowl, points downward; hold a couple seconds until cookie becomes crisp. Place in muffin cup to cool. These are a very nice texture. Makes 8.

Fortune Cookies (Baked in oven)

1/4 cup salad oil	1/4 cup sugar
1/2 cup unsifted all-purpose flour	Pinch of salt
1/4 cup egg whites (about 2)	1 teaspoon vanilla
1 tablespoon cornstarch	1 1/2 teaspoons water

Combine ingredients; beat until smooth. Spread a tablespoonful of batter on lightly greased cookie sheet to 3 1/2-inch circle for each cookie. Bake in upper third of a 300-degree oven until light brown, 15 to 20 minutes. In center place a fortune slip; fold cookie in half; remove from pan; bend over rim or cup or bowl; hold a few seconds until cookie becomes crisp. (Let baking sheet cool between each baking.)

Cakes

Angel Food Cake Pointers

Angel food cake prepared from scratch is tastier than one from a mix—and just as simple to make.

Egg whites are the key to the cake's volume, so carefully follow procedure for beating egg whites. Have whites at room temperature and beat in fat-free copper, stainless steel, or glass bowl. To remove any accidental trace of yolk from egg whites, touch yolk with small piece of bread. It will cling to bread without removing any of egg white.

Use an ungreased, straight-sided tube pan for baking the cake; the ungreased sides of pan allow batter to cling and rise to maximum height.

Cool baked cake upside down to allow structure to set without collapsing. Some pans have metal feet to make it easy to set upside down; if yours doesn't, place it over neck of bottle so air can circulate beneath it.

The weather can influence results. For maximum volume, it is best to prepare angel food cake during dry weather rather than on humid or rainy days.

Angle Food Cake

1 cup sifted cake flour	1 1/4 teaspoons cream of tartar
10 egg whites	1 1/4 cups sugar, divided
1/8 teaspoon salt	1 1/2 teaspoons vanilla extract

Sift together 1/4 cup sugar and flour; set aside. Beat room-temperature egg whites until foamy. Add cream of tartar and salt; beat until soft peaks form. Add remaining sugar, 2 tablespoons at a time, beating until stiff peaks form. Sift flour mixture over egg white mixture, 1/4 cup at a time; fold in; fold in vanilla.

Spoon batter into an ungreased 10-inch tube pan, spreading evenly. Break large air pockets by cutting through batter with a knife. Bake at 350 degrees until cake springs back when lightly touched, about 40 minutes. Invert pan; cool at least 40 minutes. Loosen cake from sides of pan using a narrow metal spatula; remove from pan. Serves 12.

Favorite Chocolate Cake

1/2 cup Crisco®	1 3/4 cups all-purpose flour
1/2 cup granulated sugar	1/4 cup cornstarch
1/2 cup brown sugar	2 teaspoons baking powder
2 eggs	2 squares unsweetened chocolate
1 cup buttermilk	1/2 teaspoon soda
1/4 teaspoon salt	1 teaspoon vanilla

Sift and measure flour; add salt, baking powder, soda and sift 3 times. Carefully melt chocolate in custard cup in microwave oven. Combine Crisco®, sugars and eggs; beat until light and creamy; stir in melted chocolate; mix well. Stir in vanilla, buttermilk, and sifted flour mixture; beat until blended. Pour into a greased and floured rectangular baking pan or 2 (8-inch) cake tins. Bake in 350 degree oven 35 to 40 minutes. Cake will pull very slightly away from sides of pan when done. Cool a few minutes before removing from pan; or frost in pan, if desired.

Seven-Minute Frosting

1/3 cup water	1 tablespoon corn syrup
2 eggs	1 1/2 cups sugar
Dash of salt	1 teaspoon vanilla
3 or 4 tablespoons powdered sugar	

Combine water, egg whites, corn syrup, and sugar in top of a double boiler over boiling water. Beat at high speed until frosting forms soft peaks. Remove from heat and beat until frosting forms stiff peaks. Beat in 3 or 4 tablespoons sifted powdered sugar to make an easy spreading frosting. Beat in vanilla.

Pineapple Upside-Down Cake (Delicious)

2 tablespoons butter	1 cup sifted flour
3/4 cup brown sugar	1/4 teaspoon salt
6 rings sliced pineapple	1 teaspoon baking powder
2 eggs, well beaten	1/2 cup boiling water
1 cup granulated sugar	1 teaspoon vanilla

Spread brown sugar over melted butter in cast-iron skillet; then arrange pineapple slices over top. To well-beaten eggs, add cup of granulated sugar; beat until light; add sifted dry ingredients; stir in vanilla and boiling water; beat 1/2 minute. Pour batter over pineapple slices. Bake in preheated 375-degree oven about 25 minutes. Let stand 5 minutes. Cover skillet with serving plate; invert; shake gently then lift pan. Serve cake warm topped with whipped cream.

To make individuals: Divide brown sugar and butter among five 10-ounce oven-proof cups; place a pineapple ring on top. Divide the prepared batter among cups. Bake until nicely browned. Turn upside down on individual dessert plates. Serve warm with whipped cream, centered with a cherry.

"Best Ever" Prune Cake

1/4 cup butter	2 1/2 cups sifted flour
1/4 cup Crisco®	2 teaspoons baking powder
1 1/2 cups sugar	1 pint stewed prunes, cut fine
3 eggs, separated	1 teaspoon vanilla
1 teaspoon soda	1/4 teaspoon salt
1/2 cup buttermilk	1 cup chopped nuts

Heat together butter, Crisco®, egg yolks, and vanilla until light. Stir in sifted dry ingredients alternately with buttermilk. Add prunes and nuts; blending well. Fold in stiffly beaten egg whites and salt. Bake in oiled and floured loaf cake pan about 30 minutes at 350 degrees. Ice or frost as desired using Sea Foam Frosting (next page).

Prize-Winning Spice Nut Cake

1/2 cup Crisco®	2 cups sifted cake flour
3/4 cup brown sugar	1/2 teaspoon soda
1/2 cup granulated sugar	2 teaspoons baking powder
2 eggs	1/8 teaspoon salt
1 cup buttermilk	1 teaspoon cinnamon
1 teaspoon vanilla	1/2 teaspoon cloves
1/2 cup chopped pecans	1/4 teaspoon nutmeg

Cream shortening, sugar, and eggs together until light and fluffy. Add sifted dry ingredients alternately with milk and vanilla; beat well. Fold in nuts. Pour batter into two buttered and lightly floured 8-inch round cake tins. Bake at 365 degrees about 25 minutes. Frost layers with Sea Foam Frosting and spread an inch-wide circle of chopped nutmeats around edge of frosting.

Sea Foam Frosting

1 cup dark corn syrup	2 tablespoons strong coffee
1/2 cup brown sugar	2 stiffly beaten eggs whites
1/4 teaspoon salt	

Combine the dark corn syrup, brown sugar, salt, and coffee. Cook to thread stage (230 degrees). Gradually pour over the egg whites, beating constantly. Continue beating until of spreading consistency.

Desserts

Quick and Delicious Baked Banana

If you are a banana fan—like them fresh and unadorned, eaten fresh sliced over cereals, in salads, in ice cream and sorbets, you'll love them cooked. Sautéed, broiled, or baked, they develop a new taste flavor.

Allow one banana for each person. Slice each banana in half lengthwise; place on lightly buttered baking dish, cut side up. Sprinkle tops with a little brown sugar. Bake in a 375-degree oven until lightly browned, 15 to 20 minutes. Serve topped with a spoonful whipped cream or ice cream.

Buttery Bananas, Stove-Top Method

2 large bananas, peeled, sliced in half lengthwise

2 tablespoons butter

3 tablespoons brown sugar

4 teaspoons rum or orange juice

1 teaspoon vanilla extract

vanilla ice cream

chopped pecans, optional

Melt butter in nonstick skillet; add brown sugar, rum or orange juice, and vanilla. Cook, stirring constantly, over low heat, until sugar dissolves. Add banana halves and cook 2 to 3 minutes. Place bananas on two dessert plates; top with vanilla ice cream and pour sauce over. Garnish with chopped pecans, if desired. Serve immediately.

Cantaloupe á la Mode

2 small cantaloupes, chilled

1 pint French vanilla ice cream or ice milk

10 ounces frozen strawberries, barely thawed

Cut melons in half; scoop out seeds. Place on chilled individual dessert plates; fill each with scoop of ice cream and top with strawberries. Serve immediately. Serves 4.

Cherries Jubilee

Cherries Jubilee is a spectacular dessert, invented by the great Escoffier in honor of Queen Victoria's Jubilee.

1 tablespoon cornstarch	1 pound can pitted black cherries
1 tablespoon sugar	1/4 teaspoon almond flavoring
Pint of vanilla ice cream	1/4 cup warm brandy or kirsch

Divide ice cream among 4 to 6 chilled dessert dishes; set dishes in freezer compartment of refrigerator.

Mix cornstarch, and sugar together; add liquid from canned cherries; stir until smooth; bring to boiling, stirring constantly, cook 2 minutes. Stir in cherries and almond flavoring; heat through. Heat brandy or kirsch in small container until bubbles form around edge of pan. Ignite with match; pour over cherry mixture. Serve flaming over vanilla ice cream. Serves 4 to 6.

Wonderful Double-Boiler Bread Pudding

1 cup brown sugar	2 cups milk
3 slices bread	1/4 cup raisins
2 tablespoons butler	1 teaspoon vanilla
3 eggs	Pinch of salt

Butter bread slices and cut into small cubes. Butter inside of double boiler top; spread in brown sugar; cover with bread cubes; sprinkle raisins on top. Beat eggs, milk, salt, and vanilla; pour mixture over ingredients in double boiler—do not stir. Cover and simmer water for 1 hour. Serve hot. Delicious. Serves 6.

Brown Rice Custard

2 eggs	1 14 1/2 ounce can evaporated
1/3 cup brown sugar	milk, undiluted
1/2 teaspoon salt	1/2 cup water
1 teaspoon vanilla	2 cups cooked quick brown rice
1/2 cup chopped dates	Nutmeg

Beat eggs lightly with sugar, salt, and vanilla. Stir in milk, water, rice, and dates. Turn into shallow 1 1/2 quart baking dish, and sprinkle generously with nutmeg. Set in pan of hot water. Bake in moderate oven (350 degrees) about 45 minutes, until knife inserted in custard comes out clean. Serves 6.

Caramel Custard Cups (The sauce bakes with the custard.)

1 cup evaporated milk

2/3 cup water

1/4 cup sugar

1/4 cup brown sugar

2 eggs, slightly beaten

1 teaspoon vanilla

Press 1 tablespoon of brown sugar in each of 4 lightly buttered custard cups to cover bottoms completely.

Blend together eggs, milk, water, 1/4 cup sugar, vanilla, and salt. Carefully pour mixture over brown sugar. Set cups in shallow pan holding 1 inch of hot water; set in oven and bake in preheated 325-degree oven about 45 minutes, or until knife inserted near edge of custard comes out clean even though custard might still be a touch wiggly. Cool, but do not chill; loosen edges with a knife; unmold upside down in dessert dishes. Top with teaspoonful of whipped cream and a cherry for color. Very nice. Serves 4.

Meringue Shells

3/4 cup sugar

1 teaspoon vanilla

Pinch of salt

3 egg whites, room temperature

1/4 teaspoon cream of tartar

Beat egg whites with salt and cream of tartar until foamy. Gradually add sugar, beating until stiff and glossy. Add vanilla. Drop meringue by 1/2 cups onto parchment-paper-lined (or brown-paper-lined) baking sheet, a few inches apart. Using back of spoon, shape mounds into circles, building up sides.

Bake at 275 degrees 1 hour. Turn off oven. Leave meringues in oven with door closed at least 1 1/2 hours. Remove from oven and cool away from drafts. Makes 4 to 9 shells.

Overnight Meringue Shells

1 1/4 cups sugar

Pinch of salt

1 teaspoon vanilla

4 egg whites, room temperature

1/4 teaspoon cream of tartar

1 teaspoon lemon juice

Beat egg whites, cream of tartar, and salt until soft peaks form; gradually beat in sugar. Beat until stiff and glossy; beat in lemon juice and vanilla. Cover large baking sheet with sheet of brown paper; spoon on and shape 8 meringue cups 2 inches apart.

Place on middle rack in a preheated 450-degree oven; close door. After 1 minute, turn off heat; leave meringues in oven overnight. These meringues will be crisp and tender. Do not let them absorb moisture.

To serve, place meringue shells on individual dessert plates; fill with large scoop of vanilla ice cream; top with slightly sweetened fresh or frozen, sliced strawberries. Very special!

Baked Alaska

Baked Alaska was supposedly invented at New York's legendary Delmonico restaurant to celebrate the purchase of the Territory of Alaska. It is an elegant dessert and not complicated to make. Actually it is just a cake base, topped with ice cream, covered with a meringue, and delicately browned. Serving is easy, too, because the sliced cake base and ice cream can be assembled ahead of time; then frozen.

Most any type cake can be used for the base—sponge, angel food, pound cake; store-bought or homemade. An Apple-Upside Down cake is a favorite. The slices for base should be about 1 inch thick. Freeze.

Use your favorite flavor of ice cream. The ice cream should be cut 2-inches thick and cut slightly smaller all around than the cake base. Place ice cream slices on cake and freeze.

About 10 minutes before ready to serve, prepare the meringue. Place cake base on brown-paper-covered baking sheet; top with ice cream; and quickly frost with meringue, spreading down to cover base completely. Sprinkle top with sifted powdered sugar. Bake in preheated 500-degree oven on rack in upper one-third of oven, until golden brown. Serve immediately.

Baked Alaska may be made as one, sliced and served after browning, or made as individuals. Individuals take longer to prepare but are easier to serve and are more spectacular. Individual Baked Alaskas, each topped with a lighted candle, are very special served to guests as a finale to a birthday dinner.

For each individual Baked Alaska, allow 1 egg white, pinch of salt, pinch of cream of tartar, 2 tablespoons powdered sugar, and 1/4 teaspoon vanilla. For one large Alaska for 6 people, allow 5 large egg whites, pinch or salt 1/4 teaspoon cream of tartar, 2/3 cup powdered sugar (or granulated sugar, or brown sugar), and 1 teaspoon vanilla.

Baked Alaska Quickie

Cut a rectangular Angel Food Cake crosswise into 1-inch thick slices; chill. Cut 2-inch thick slices of ice cream slightly smaller than width of cake slice; chill. The sliced cake will be enough for 6 people. Place ice cream slices on top of cake base; cover quickly with meringue. Sprinkle top with powdered sugar; bake in preheated 500-degree oven until golden brown, about 2 minutes. Serve immediately.

To-Each-His-Own Baked Alaska (Cake base, using the egg yolks)

3/8	cup Crisco®	1 1/8	cups sifted flour
3/4	cup sugar	3	teaspoons baking powder
6	egg yolks, beaten		Pinch of salt
3/8	cup milk	1	teaspoon vanilla

Combine Crisco®, sugar, and vanilla; beat until light. Add well-beaten egg yolks. Add sifted dry ingredients and milk; thoroughly mix; then spoon batter into buttered and floured 4- or 5-inch individual baking dishes, filling no more than 1/4 to 1/3 full. Bake foil at 400 degrees; glass at 375 degrees for 20 minutes. Makes 6 to 8 individual cakes. Set for a couple minutes then remove and cool completely on wire racks. Can be made ahead of time and frozen.

Ice Cream

A day ahead of time, divide about a quart of ice cream into 6 or 8 (5-ounce) custard cups; press in firmly and level off tops; freeze. When frozen, remove from cups (hold each upside down under hot water faucet for a couple seconds); place on foil and freeze until ready to use. You can put 1 1/2 tablespoons crushed pineapple or crushed strawberries in each custard cup, then fill cup with vanilla ice cream for a change.

Meringue

6	egg whites	1/4	teaspoon cream of tartar
1/4	teaspoon salt	3/4	cup powdered sugar
1	teaspoon vanilla		

Place frozen cakes on brown paper on baking sheet, allowing enough distance between so meringues will not touch. Place frozen ice cream on top of each.

Beat egg whites, salt, and cream of tartar until soft peaks form; gradually add sugar; beat until stiff and glossy, not dry; add vanilla. Quickly cover the ice cream with the meringue, sealing at the base of the cake.

Place on rack in upper third of a preheat 500-degree oven; bake until a golden brown, about 2 minutes. With spatula, place each on individual plates. Serve immediately.

Note: To avoid the rush between the main course and dessert, after the meringue has been spread on, completely covering each, place in freezer. Do this just a few minutes before dinner is served. Then just before dessert, slip into preheated oven and bake.

Colonial Floating Island

Floating Island is a classic; the ingredients are simple—eggs, cream or milk, and sugar; the presentation is impressive; and taste is more sophisticated than recipe indicates.

Floating Island is appropriately named. Puffs of velvety meringues rest on a smooth custard sauce.

Floating Island was called "Snow Eggs" in Colonial times. And originally this recipe called for poaching the egg white mixture in the milk and then using the milk to make a custard in the double boiler. Now people prepare the white mixture in various ways: poaching in milk, poaching over water, baking in oven, etc. However it is made, "Floating Island" is a special treat; looks as good as it tastes.

Poached Meringues

2 egg whites	3 cups milk
Dash of salt	1/4 cup sugar

Beat egg whites with dash of salt until soft peaks form. Gradually add the sugar, beating to stiff peaks. In a skillet heat the milk to a simmer. Drop meringue in by tablespoonsful to make 6 meringues. Cook slowly, uncovered, until firm, about 5 minutes. Lift from milk (use milk in custard); drain on paper towels; remove to wax paper on cookie sheet. Chill.

Custard

3 eggs	Dash of salt
2 egg yolks	2 1/2 cups strained milk
1/3 cup sugar	1 1/2 teaspoons vanilla

Beat eggs and egg yolks slightly; stir in sugar and salt. Stir in slightly cooled milk (should be about 2 1/2 cups from meringues). Strain into top of double boiler. Cook over hot, but not boiling water, stirring constantly, until mixture coats a metal spoon. At once, remove from heat; cool slightly; add vanilla Chill over ice water; then pour into chilled serving dish. Top with chilled meringues.

For variety: Pour custard equally into 6 sauce dishes; chill. To serve, place chilled meringue on top of each.

Prune Whip (An old favorite)

Cooked or canned prunes	2 envelops unflavored gelatin
1 1/2 cups prune juice	1/2 cup sugar or to taste
1 teaspoon vanilla	1 cup heavy cream, whipped

Drain cooked or canned prunes; remove pits and purée in electric blender to make 1 cup; chill. Soak gelatin in 1/2 cup of the prune juice; then dissolve in the cup of heated prune juice and sugar. Add vanilla and a little lemon juice, if desired. Chill until mixture is thick but not firm; whip with electric mixer until light and fluffy; add chilled prune pulp; beat thoroughly; carefully fold in whipped cream. Chill in dessert glasses until ready to serve. To serve, top with spoonful of whipped cream garnished with chopped pecans.

Baked Prune Whip

1 1/2 cups cooked, drained prunes	1/2 teaspoon grated orange peel
1 1/2 teaspoon lemon juice	4 tablespoons sugar, divided
4 egg whites	1/4 teaspoon cream of tartar
Pinch of salt	

Purée prunes; blend in orange peel and lemon juice, and 1 tablespoon sugar; set aside.

Beat egg whites, cream of tartar, and salt to form soft peaks; gradually add remaining 3 tablespoons sugar, beating until stiff peaks form. Fold in prune mixture. Pile lightly into a 12- by 8-inch baking dish. Place dish in a large roasting pan on oven rack and fill pan with water halfway up side of dish. Bake in 350-degree oven 30 to 35 minutes. Serve warm with whipped cream or a Custard Sauce. (Or serve plain.) Serves 6.

Custard Sauce

2 cups half-and-half
Dash of salt
1 1/2 teaspoons vanilla

4 egg yolks, beaten
1/4 cup sugar

Beat egg yolks, sugar, and salt together until light; stir in cream. In top of double boiler over simmering water, cook, stirring constantly, until mixture coats metal spoon. Remove from heat; stir in vanilla. Cover with cloth (to absorb the moisture that collects inside the lid) and plastic wrap; refrigerate until cool. Makes 2 cups.

Soufflés

When making a soufflé, meringues, or any other recipe that calls for stiffly beaten egg whites, remember to part the yolks from the white while the eggs are cold—right from the refrigerator. Then get rest of ingredients together so whites can warm to room temperature before beating. Adding a small amount of cream of tartar will help react to protein, or albumen, in egg whites and stabilize the whites so they will incorporate more air in beating.

Classic Hot Soufflé

The classic dessert souffle is made from a base of rich pastry cream, which can be flavored with your favorite liqueur. It is lightened with stiffly beaten egg whites before being put into oven, where it rises to form a crown high above the mold.

A pastry cream (the cream used in eclairs, napoleons, and cream puffs and for bases of many fruit tarts) is made by combining milk, flour, sugar, and egg yolks and cooking them until a smooth, thick, and creamy sauce is formed. When properly cooked and cooled, it's ready for the egg whites. Since the soufflé base is usually thicker and heavier than the beaten whites, about a third of the beaten whites should be folded in first; this portion of the batter will deflate substantially, but it will lighten the base so remaining egg whites can be incorporated easily and retain maximum volume. The folding action should be quick and gentle, just until no more streaks of white are visible.

Then pour into a lightly buttered, sugar-coated mold. There should be just enough mixture to fill mold evenly or slightly above rim. Gently smoothing top of soufflé and running thumb around edge of

dish to clean off edge helps soufflé to rise straight up in a "high hat" effect rather than doming and perhaps breaking in the middle. Bake according to recipe instructions.

When correctly baked, this classic custard-base soufflé is relatively firm on the outside, but remains soft and creamy at the center. If a drier, firmer soufflé is preferred, as many people do, just leave the soufflé in oven a few minutes longer.

A soufflé scares and amazes more cooks than almost any other main dish. And yet, it is rather simple to make. But keep in mind, a soufflé does not wait for dinner guests; they must wait for the soufflé. It must be served immediately when taken from the oven.

Soufflé dishes must be ovenproof and should have straight sides to promote even cooking. When using glassware for baking, reduce oven temperature by 25 degrees.

Be precise in your measurements; follow directions for mixing and baking, and you can create a soufflé that will impress your friends.

A soufflé is a combination of a flavored foundation and stiffly beaten egg whites, which make it rise. The foundation may be either a flavored roux or a fruit purée. Almost any food can flavor the roux—cheese, mushrooms, chicken, salmon, clams, corn, spinach, chocolate, orange, etc.—and nearly any type of fruit can be puréed. Timing must be exact so mixture bakes to the perfect consistency and height.

When preparing a soufflé, always cook the roux before beating the egg whites. It can afford to wait, the egg whites cannot. Allow roux to cool to lukewarm.

Always begin with room-temperature egg whites. Many cooks prefer to beat the egg whites with a wire whisk, because the air is kept circulating throughout the entire mass of egg whites and thus increases the volume.

If you are using an electric mixer, the best procedure is to start at a low speed and gradually increase to high until whites are stiff.

A perfect soufflé is created with whites that are stiff but not dry. This frequently stated terminology means that the whites are beaten to glossy peaks that have a moist appearance and cling to the whip or beater. If whites are whipped beyond this point to the dry stage, they become granular, are difficult to work with, and break when folded into the base.

Fold a small portion of egg whites into roux, just enough to combine. Then add this mixture to remaining egg whites. Lightly fold egg whites and roux, but be careful not to overmix.

Soufflés should be set on lower oven rack to bake.

Hot Chocolate Soufflé   (An old favorite)

1/2 cup sugar	3 squares unsweetened chocolate
3 tablespoons flour	2 tablespoons butter
4 egg yolks	6 egg whites
1 cup milk	1/4 teaspoon cream of tartar
Pinch of salt	1 teaspoon vanilla

Butter and sugar-coat a 2-quart soufflé dish or casserole. Set aside. Set oven at 350 degrees.

Blend 6 tablespoons of the sugar with flour and salt in top of double boiler; work in butter and chocolate; gradually stir in milk. Stir until mixture thickens and is smooth; remove from heat; stir in vanilla; cool slightly. Beat egg yolks until light; blend in slightly cooled chocolate mixture. Beat egg whites and cream of tartar in large bowl until soft peaks form when beater is raised; add remaining 2 tablespoons sugar slowly; beat until stiff. Stir about 1/4 of egg white mixture into chocolate mixture; then carefully fold in remaining egg whites. Pour into prepared baking dish; sprinkle top lightly with sugar.

Bake at 350 degrees about 50 minutes until light and puffy. Serve immediately with ice-cold whipped cream, a custard sauce, a warm chocolate sauce, or just plain. (Let guests help themselves.) Serves 6 to 8.

Hot Chocolate Soufflé for Four

5 tablespoons brown sugar	1/8 teaspoon cream of tartar
3 egg yolks	2 tablespoons + 3/4 teaspoon flour
3/4 cup milk	1 1/2 tablespoons butter
2 1/2 squares unsweetened chocolate	1 tablespoon sugar
4 1/2 egg whites (9 tablespoons)	1 teaspoon vanilla

Butter and sugar-coat a 1 1/2-inch deep soufflé dish or casserole, or four 20-ounce individual dishes. Set aside. Then proceed to prepare as for "Hot Chocolate Souffle" above. It will take a little less time to bake; bake until puffed and golden brown. Serve immediately with a bowl of whipped cream on the side.

Cocoa Mocha Soufflé

3/4 teaspoon butter	1 teaspoon instant coffee
1/2 tablespoon sugar	1 teaspoon vanilla
1 tablespoon cornstarch	1/2 teaspoon orange liqueur
1 1/2 tablespoons sugar	3 egg whites
2 tablespoons cocoa	Pinch of salt
1/2 cup milk	1/4 teaspoon cream of tartar

Butter and sugar-coat a 1-quart casserole. Place rack in lower 1/3 of oven; preheat oven to 425 degrees.

Sift together cornstarch, 1 1/2 tablespoons sugar, 2 tablespoons cocoa, and coffee powder; stir in milk; stir over medium heat until sauce thickens. Remove from heat; stir in liqueur and vanilla. Beat egg whites, salt, and cream of tartar until stiff; beat in 1/2 tablespoon sugar; fold 1/3 into sauce; then carefully fold in remaining whites. Turn into prepared dish; smooth top. With finger, remove about 1/4-inch batter around edge of dish so crown rises straight.

Place in oven. After about 5 minutes, reduce temperature to 375 degrees. Bake until puffed and dark golden. Serve immediately. Serves 4.

Tapioca

Those gelatinous pearls of tapioca are a starch from the root of the tropical cassava or manioc plant. To reach edible form, the toxic root is washed, peeled, and leached of its toxins, then finely ground. Repeated washing and draining follow. As the starch washes out, it is collected, dried, then pulverized to make a fine flour.

Pearl tapioca, large or small, is made from the flour mixed with water. The resulting dough is shaped into pellets and toasted on griddle to create a hard shell. Pellets are then dried thoroughly. These hard beads need to be soaked several hours before cooking.

Quick-cooking tapioca is a mixture of tapioca flour and water that is cooked, dried, and then ground again to make small, even pieces. The precooking and granular size make your preparation time considerably shorter.

One of tapioca's great attributes is its ability to hold moisture. When heated in liquid, particles swell and become transparent. Use the flour and quick-cooking and small-pearl tapiocas as you would corn-starch—as thickeners. Stir only until your mixture boils; stirring after boiling may make tapioca mixtures stringy.

Tapioca flour renders a smooth, clear sauce. Quick-cooking and small-pearl tapiocas swell and become clear but retain their shape. All three forms perform well in juicy fruit pies.

Because of its size, the large-pearl tapioca is less effective for thickening and is best used when you want to add a chewy, bouncy texture—perhaps to a pudding.

Years ago the large pearl tapioca was the only type sold. The instant tapioca has replaced the large pearl tapioca on the grocery shelves—rarely is the large type available.

Large Pearl Tapioca Pudding

1/2	cup tapioca	2	tablespoons brown sugar
2	cups milk	2	eggs, separated
	Pinch of salt	1	teaspoon vanilla

Place milk in top of double boiler; bring to a simmer; stir in taprioca, 1 1/2 tablespoons brown sugar and pinch of salt. Cook covered over simmering water about 30 minutes stirring a few times to keep tapioca from becoming lumpy. When transparent, beat yolks and remaining sugar with tablespoon milk; stir a little of heated mixture into yolk mixture to blend; then stir into hot mixture. Heat, without boiling, stirring, just until mixture starts to thicken. Beat egg whites until stiff; gradually beat in remaining sugar and vanilla. Fold whites into tapioca mixture. Delicious served hot with cream. But also good served chilled, topped with whipped cream or ice cream. Serves 4.

Minute Tapioca Pudding

2	cups milk	3	tablespoons minute tapioca
3	tablespoons sugar	2	egg whites
2	egg yolks	2	tablespoons sugar
	Pinch of salt	1	teaspoon vanilla

Heat the milk (may use 1 cup evaporated milk and 1 cup water) holding out 2 tablespoons; add tapioca, stirring until tapioca starts to cook; then cover and cook about 3 minutes, or until tapioca is transparent. In a cup, mix 3 tablespoons sugar, salt, and egg yolks; stir in a few tablespoons of hot mixture to blend. Stir egg mixture into hot mixture; stir until custard consistency. Remove from heat. Beat egg whites until fluffy; beat in the 2 tablespoons sugar and vanilla. Carefully fold whites into custard mixture. Serve slightly cooled with cream or chill and top with whipped cream garnished with a cherry. Serves 4.

Microwaved Minute Tapioca Pudding

2 cups milk	3 tablespoons brown sugar
2 egg yolks	2 egg whites
Pinch of salt	2 tablespoon brown sugar
1 teaspoon vanilla	

Place milk (minus 2 tablespoons) in 4 cup dish. Cover; set in microwave on HIGH. As soon as it comes to boil, stir in tapioca. Bring to boil (watch carefully so it doesn't boil over); stir and bring to boil a couple times or more until tapioca is transparent. Beat yolks and 2 tablespoons milk, 3 tablespoons brown sugar; stir; blend in a little of hot mixture, then stir into tapioca mixture; barely simmer, stir a couple times until starting to thicken. Careful, don't overcook or custard will separate. Remove from heat, stir. Beat egg whites; beat in salt, sugar and vanilla. Fold beaten whites into custard. Serve warm with cream or cover with a cloth and lid and chill in refrigerator. Serve topped with whipped cream garnished with a maraschino cherry.

Pies

Pie Crusts

There are many recipes for pie crusts. For a starter, "Foolproof Flaky Pie Crust" is easy to handle. And "Never-Fail Pie Crust" is wonderful dough to have on hand. In preparing the pastry dough it is important not to overhandle or use too much flour in rolling. Roll pastry out on lightly floured work surface to a circle 1/16 to 1/8-inch thick. Roll lightly and quickly, periodically lifting dough and dusting work surface with flour to prevent dough from sticking. To avoid shrinking of pie crust, roll dough large enough to ease into the pie plate, never pull or stretch. Gently press bottom and sides of dough against pan. For one-crust pies, trim edges, leaving 1/2 inch overhanging; turn under and crimp edges. Lightly prick bottom and sides of pastry so in baking crust will hold its shape. For two-crusted pies, do not prick bottom crust; moisten overhanging pastry and cover filling with top crust pressing edges to seal; turn under sealed edges and crimp. Slit top to let steam escape in baking.

Bake an unfilled pie shell quickly in middle of an upper shelf of the oven, but bake a double-crusted pie on a lower shelf where the bottom crust will set faster. If crust begins to brown too quickly on the top of edges, cover loosely with a circle of foil around edges.

Foolproof Flaky Pie Crust

The formula: Use half as much shortening as flour, and half as much water as shortening, and a dash of salt for luck.

1/2 cup Crisco®	1 cup all-purpose flour
Pinch of salt	1/4 cup ice water

This is enough for a two-crusted pie. Cut in shortening until flour and shortening look like coarse meal; mix in water. Divide dough in half. Roll on well-floured board. Keep rolling from the middle and don't go over the edge every time or edge gets too thin.

Flaky Crust

1 cup all-purpose flour	3 tablespoons Crisco®
1/8 teaspoon salt	3 or 4 tablespoons milk
3 tablespoons cold butter	

In medium bowl, combine flour and salt. Cut in butter and Crisco® until mixture resembles coarse crumbs. Add milk, 1 tablespoon at a time, mixing with fork until dough just sticks together. Press into ball. Roll out on lightly floured surface into 10-inch circle. Carefully fit into 9-inch pie plate. Trim edges; flute as desired. Prick bottom and side of pastry with fork. Bake in preheated 425-degree oven 10 minutes or until lightly browned. Cool completely on wire rack.

Never-Fail Pie Crust   (Favorite to have on hand)

3 cups sifted flour	4 to 6 tablespoons ice water
1/4 teaspoon salt	1 tablespoon vinegar
1 1/4 cups Crisco®	1 egg
1 tablespoon sugar, optional	

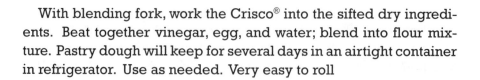

With blending fork, work the Crisco® into the sifted dry ingredients. Beat together vinegar, egg, and water; blend into flour mixture. Pastry dough will keep for several days in an airtight container in refrigerator. Use as needed. Very easy to roll

Apple Pie

To make the difference between good and great, substitute light brown sugar for granulated in your apple pie to really perk up flavor.

3 cups sliced apples	1/2 teaspoon cinnamon
1 teaspoon butter	1/3 to 1/2 cup brown sugar
1 teaspoon flour	I teaspoon strawberry Jell-O®

Prepare your favorite pie dough for a 2-crust pie. Roll out bottom crust and fit into 8- or 9-inch pie pan. Combine sugar, pinch of salt, flour, cinnamon, and Jell-O® in bowl. Sprinkle 2 tablespoons mixture over bottom crust. Combine remaining mixture with sliced apples; turn into crust; dot with butter. Moisten edges of lower crust; fit over top crust; trim and crimp edges to seal. Cut vents for steam to escape. For glazed top, brush crust with cream, or 1 tablespoon milk and teaspoon brown sugar, or evaporated milk; sprinkle lightly with sugar. Bake on lower shelf in preheated 450-degree oven for 10 minutes. Then move pie to center shelf, reduce heat to 350 degrees and continue to bake 30 to 40 minutes until juice starts to show and crust is nicely browned.

To prevent the top crust edge from over browning, cover with a strip of aluminum foil the last part of cooking.

Blueberry Plum Pie

Prepare dough for a two-crusted pie. Prepare the frozen filling:

1 cup sliced, peeled, ripe plums	2 1/2 cups blueberries
1/2 cup brown sugar	1 tablespoon flour
2 tablespoons lemon Jell-O®	

Combine sugar, Jell-O®, and flour. Set aside. Peel and slice plums; add blueberries. Carefully blend in sugar mixture. Pour mixture into a plastic-wrap-lined 8-inch pie plate; lightly fold wrap over top and freeze. When frozen, remove from pan, wrap airtight, and put in freezer.

To Bake: Brush the top of the thinly rolled bottom crust lightly with butter and chill a few minutes; then sprinkle with a little brown sugar. Remove wrapper and fit frozen filling into pie shell. Lightly sprinkle a little sugar over top. Wet edges of pastry and seal on top crust; cut slits in top crust. Lightly sprinkle a little sugar over top. Bake on bottom shelf in 425-degree oven. If top crust browns too quickly, cover rim with a cut-out circle of aluminum foil. Bake until golden and juice starts to bubble, about 40 minutes

Note: Adding some powdered vanilla to the sugar mixture in filling adds a delicious flavor too.

Favorite Fresh Strawberry Pie

4	cup fresh strawberries	3-ounce pkg. strawberry Jell-O®
3/4	cup sugar	9-inch pastry shell
3/4	cup boiling water	Whipping cream for topping

Wash, stem, drain, sweeten, and chill the ripe, fresh berries. Dissolve the Jell-O® in boiling water. Quick-cool over ice water, stirring often, until thick syrupy mixture is almost set; pour over chilled sweetened berries; blend carefully so all berries are well coated. Spoon gently into chilled pie crust. Chill. Serve topped with sweetened whipped cream. Note: Use any berry or fruit of your preference that is ripe; use Jell-O® flavor to suit the fruit.

Chocolate Pie   (Teeder's favorite)

Baked pie crust

8 small Hershey's® Special Dark® chocolate bars

18 large marshmallows

1/2 cup whipping cream

1 cup whipping cream

Melt chocolate bars, marshmallows, and 1/2 cup whipping cream together. Let cool.

Whip 1 cup whipping cream; fold into cooled chocolate mixture. Pour into cooled pie shell and refrigerate.

Serve topped with curls of chocolate and slivered nuts.

Kahlua® Pecan Cream Pie (Special)

1/4 cup butter	1/2 cup corn syrup
3/4 cup brown sugar	3/4 cup evaporated milk
1 teaspoon vanilla	7/8 cup chopped pecans
2 tablespoons flour	9-inch pastry crust
3 eggs	1/2 cup whipping cream
1/2 cup Kahlua®	

Line a 9-inch pie plate with your favorite pastry recipe; chill. Cream together butter, sugar, vanilla, and flour; add eggs and beat until light. Stir in Kahlua®, corn syrup, evaporated milk, and chopped pecans; mix well. Pour filling into pie crust. Bake for 10 minutes on bottom shelf in a 400-degree preheated oven then reduce heat to 325 degrees and continue to bake about 40 to 60 minutes (on middle shelf) until firm or pie does not jiggle. Refrigerate at least 3 hours until set. To serve garnish with whipped cream, sweetened with powdered sugar and vanilla flavoring. Serves 8.

Making Perfect Meringues for Topping Pies

One of the important things to remember about pie meringues is that they must bake at a moderate temperature (350 degrees for 15 to 20 minutes until nicely browned). Lower heat will dry the meringue, and higher heat will cause the egg protein to shrink, shrivel, or "weep." Pie meringue contains a proportion of 2 tablespoons sugar for each large egg white used. (If you have a collection of egg whites in a jar, remember that one "large" egg white measures 2 tablespoons.)

Volume is an important factor in making pie meringue. Utensils should be free of grime or grease. Egg whites should be at room temperature (about 70 degrees) and contain no sign of yolk. Use the exact amount of sugar called for in the recipe. Too little sugar makes a tough meringue and too much makes a gummy one.

Heavenly Apple-Custard Meringue Pie

Use your favorite pie crust recipes Shape into a 9-inch shell or 6 individual shells. Bake. Set aside to cool.

Apple Filling

3/8 cup brown sugar	2 2/3 cups finely sliced apples
2 teaspoons cornstarch	1 tablespoon water
2 teaspoons vanilla	2 teaspoons strawberry Jell-O®

Combine apples, sugar, cornstarch, and water in casserole. Microwave, covered, about 3 minutes, stirring occasionally. Cook until apples are barely tender and mixture thickened. Stir in Jell-O and vanilla; stir to blend. Chill.

Custard

3 egg yolks	2 tablespoons cornstarch
1 3/4 cups milk	3 tablespoons brown sugar
1 teaspoon vanilla	

Beat egg yolks until light; add milk, sugar, and cornstarch. Cook until thick in top of double boiler, stirring constantly. Add the vanilla and cool.

Meringue

6 tablespoons sugar	3 egg whites, room temperature
1/4 teaspoon salt	1/4 teaspoon cream of tartar

Beat egg whites, salt, and cream of tartar until soft peaks form; gradually add sugar and cornstarch; beat until stiff and glossy.

To assemble, spread chilled applesauce over baked pie shell; pour the custard over evenly; then spread on meringue, sealing to edge. Bake at 350 degrees 15 to 20 minutes until nicely browned.

Lemon Meringue Pie
9-inch Pie Shell

1 cup sifted flour	2 tablespoons ice water
Pinch of salt	1 teaspoon vinegar
6 tablespoons Crisco®	1 egg yolk
2 teaspoons butter	1 teaspoon sugar

Pastry dough can be made night before and refrigerated in airtight container or plastic wrap. Blend Crisco® and butter into sifted dry ingredients. Beat together vinegar, egg yolks, and water; blend into dry ingredients. Refrigerate, Roll out 1/8-inch thick and fit into 9-inch pie plate. Trim edge; flute; prick bottom and sides of pastry with fork. Bake in preheated 425-degree oven until lightly browned, about 10 minutes. Cool completely on wire rack.

Filling

5/8 cup sugar	2 tablespoons orange Jell-O®
1/4 cup cornstarch	1/3 cup frozen lemonade
1 1/2 cups boiling water	concentrate, thawed
1/8 teaspoon salt, optional	3 egg yolks

In top of double boiler, stir together sugar, orange Jell-O®, and cornstarch; stir in a little of lemonade, stirring until smooth; stir in remaining lemonade and boiling water. Cook, stirring until mixture is smooth and starting to thicken. Stir in well-beaten egg yolks and continue to cook, stirring constantly 5 to 10 minutes longer. Remove from heat; cover with towel and completely cool. Pour filling into cooled pie shell; top with meringue.

Meringue

2 tablespoons sugar	3 egg whites
1 tablespoon cornstarch	1/8 teaspoon salt
1/4 cup water	6 tablespoons sugar
1 tablespoon lemon Jell-O®	

Blend water into combined cornstarch, sugar and Jell-O®, stirring, cook until thickened; cool. Beat egg whites and salt; slowly beat in the thickened combination. Spread meringue over filling. Bake in preheated 350-degree oven, on top shelf, until golden brown, about 15 minutes. Serves. Cool completely on wire rack. Serves 6.

Vanilla Cream Pie

2 cups milk	1 1/2 tablespoons cornstarch
1/3 cup sugar	3 egg whites
Pinch of salt	1/4 teaspoon cream of tartar
3 egg yolks	6 tablespoons sugar
1 1/2 teaspoons vanilla	1 teaspoon vanilla
Baked pie shell	1 teaspoon cornstarch

Combine 1/3 cup sugar, 1 1/2 tablespoons cornstarch, and a pinch of salt; stir in milk. Cook in top of double boiler over simmering water. Stir constantly until smooth and thickened; cover and let cook a few minutes while beating the egg yolks. Pour small amount of hot mixture into beaten yolks, mixing thoroughly; then stir into hot mixture. Cook, stirring four minutes longer. Stir in 1 1/2 teaspoons vanilla. Set aside while preparing the meringue. Beat egg whites with cream of tartar until whites stand in soft peaks; gradually add 6 tablespoons sugar and 1 teaspoon vanilla, beating until stiff; beat in 1 teaspoon cornstarch. Spread meringue over top of filling, sealing to edges. Bake at 350 degrees about 20 minutes until golden brown.

For variety, omit the meringue; use only 1 egg white; beat with 2 tablespoons sugar; then fold into the cooked cream filling. Spoon into prepared pie shell and chill. Serve with a border of sweetened whipped cream.

Using the Vanilla Cream Pie filling as a base, a variety of other interesting pies can be developed.

Butterscotch Pie: Substitute 1/2 cup brown sugar for the 1/3 cup regular sugar called for in cream filling.

Chocolate Cream Pie: Melt 2 squares unsweetened chocolate in milk in top of double boiler; increase sugar to 1/2 cup in cream filling.

Chocolate Wafer Crumb Cream Pie: Generously butter bottom and sides of pie plate; coat with chocolate wafer crumbs; chill while making pie filling and meringue. Beat vanilla in chocolate cream filling and spoon into prepared crumb crust. Spread on meringue and sprinkle top of meringue with 1/3 cup chocolate wafer crumbs. Bake at 350 degrees for 20 minutes.

Vanilla Wafer Crumb Cream Pie: Make a cupful of vanilla wafer crumbs and proceed as for the Chocolate Wafer Cream Pie.

Banana Cream Pie: Slice 1 or 2 bananas evenly over bottom of baked pie shell; pour the cream filling over top. Spread meringue over top and bake until golden. Or chill cream filling in crust and top with sweetened whipped cream flavored with vanilla.

Sour Cream Raisin Pie (For that special foursome occasion)

2	egg yolks	2	egg whites
1	tablespoon cornstarch		Pinch of salt
2	teaspoons lemon Jell-O®	2	tablespoons brown sugar
6	tablespoons brown sugar	1/3	cup whipping cream
1	cup light sour cream	1 1/2	tablespoons powdered sugar
2/3	cup golden raisins	1 1/2	teaspoon lemon juice
1 1/3	tablespoon water	1	teaspoon vanilla
	Never Fail Pie Crust dough		

Chop golden raisins and place in measuring cup; add the water and heat a couple seconds in microwave; stir and heat until water is almost absorbed. Raisins should be moist but not runny. Stir in vanilla. Cover and chill. Prepare "Never-Fail Pie Crust" dough; chill. This much can be done night before if you wish.

Roll pastry dough very thin for the individual pie tins. Bake on rack in lower third of 375-degree oven until lightly browned. Cool.

Combine cornstarch, sugar, and lemon Jell-O® until well blended; stir into well-beaten egg yolks; beat into cream; cook in double boiler over simmering water, stirring constantly, until smooth and thickened. Don't overcook. Remove from heat. Stir in vanilla-seasoned chopped raisins.

Beat egg whites and salt until soft peaks form; beat in brown sugar: stir into raisin mixture. Pour into 4 individual baked pie shells. Cool.

Whip the cream, whipping in the lemon juice and the 2 tablespoons of brown sugar. When stiff, spread the whipped cream around edge of pie and sprinkle top of cream lightly with ground pecans. Chill until ready to serve.

Favorite Pumpkin Pie

1 1/2	cups pumpkin	1/4	teaspoon cloves
2	eggs	1	dash of ginger
3/4	cup brown sugar	1	tablespoon sorghum
	Pinch of salt	2	teaspoons each flour and vanilla
2/3	teaspoon cinnamon	1 1/4	cups rich milk
1/8	teaspoon nutmeg		9-inch unbaked pastry shell

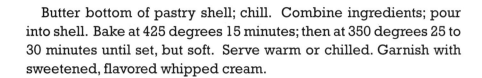

Butter bottom of pastry shell; chill. Combine ingredients; pour into shell. Bake at 425 degrees 15 minutes; then at 350 degrees 25 to 30 minutes until set, but soft. Serve warm or chilled. Garnish with sweetened, flavored whipped cream.

About the Author

Irene Buckman was born in Walla Walla, Washington in September, 1909. When she was about four, her folks bought a fifteen acre farm and started a dairy along with raising their own fruits, vegetables, animals, fowl, etc. Her mother died a month after Irene entered Walla Walla High School. So, she and her sister had to cook breakfast and the evening meal for their father, themselves and the hired men, as well as hiking to and from high school morning and evening. Her father prepared the noon meal for the men.

When she and her sister went to college (University of Washington) in 1927, her father hired a cook and housekeeper. Irene vowed she'd had enough cooking for a lifetime.

After graduation Irene taught two years at Mapleton High School in Mapleton, Oregon. She married her college sweetheart in 1933. Their son, Bruce, was born in San Bernardino, California, in 1935. The next week the family moved to Long Beach, California, where Harriet was born in 1939. In 1945 they moved to Walla Walla, buying the homestead where Irene was born.

And so from then on, they raised practically all their cooking products. Cooking then was a real challenge —they all appreciated the variety of menus and constant experimenting with the foods they raised.

Irene started to teach business subjects at Walla Walla High School when Bruce started high school. She saw both Bruce and Harriet through school and taught two more years. She quit teaching when Frank became ill with cancer and subsequently died in 1968. They were a very close family and his death was hard to accept. For the next four years Irene went on "food trips" to other countries, one outstanding food and culture tour of Europe which really encouraged her to begin filing recipes and experimenting in earnest.

In 1974 Irene bought a home in Leisure World, Laguna Hills, California. There she amassed 27 volumes of recipes, information, and ideas filed by subject. She'd often have different friends sample a new recipe she had worked on and ask for their opinions.

So with duplicate bridge, cooking challenges, close family and friends, life was rewarding. Near the close of 1996, she moved to Seattle, Washington, to live with her daughter, Harriet, who talked her into publishing this book.

Index

Order Form

Qty.	Title	Price	Can. Price	Total
	Keepsake Recipes and Fascinating Food Facts	$14.95	$18.95	
	Shipping and handling (US orders add $2.50 for first book, $2.00 for each additonal book)			
	Please call 1-800-461-1931 for international rates.			
	Sales tax (WA residents only, add 8.6%.)			
	Total enclosed			

Telephone orders:
Call 1-800-461-1931.
Have your VISA or
MasterCard ready.

E–Mail orders:
E–mail your order request
to harapub@foxinternet.net

Fax orders:
Fax completed order form
to (425) 672-8597.

Payment: Please check one
❑ Check
❑ Visa
❑ MasterCard

Postal orders:
Send completed order
form to
Hara Publishing
P.O. Box 19732
Seattle, WA 98109.

Name on Card: _____

Card #: _____

Expiration Date: _____

Name _____

Address _____

City _____ State _____ Zip _____

Daytime Phone (_____) _____

Quantity discounts are available.
For more information, call (425) 776-3390.

Thank you for your order!